THE GREAT AMERICAN
CREDIT SECRET
2

The Great American Credit Secret 2

Business Credit in the Age of AI

Antoine Sallis

Published by Game Changer Publishing

Paperback ISBN: 978-1-966659-19-8

Hardcover ISBN: 978-1-966659-06-8

Digital ISBN: 978-1-966659-07-5

GC GAME CHANGER
PUBLISHING
www.GameChangerPublishing.com

DEDICATION

I want to dedicate this book to my mom,
who taught me to keep going no matter what.

THE GREAT AMERICAN CREDIT SECRET

2

BUSINESS CREDIT IN THE AGE OF AI

ANTOINE SALLIS

CONTENTS

INTRODUCTION
THE POWER OF AI IN BUSINESS

AI IS THE FUTURE OF BUSINESS

In the tech industry, Artificial Intelligence is more than just a phrase of the moment. Future business practices will undoubtedly adopt this approach. It's time to get a new perspective on artificial intelligence if you still believe it belongs in a science fiction film. If you are not on the flight, you will fall behind when it takes off. In the current environment, being able to use AI can help you accomplish almost anything five to ten times faster. This is applicable for both private and professional purposes. Some would argue that artificial intelligence (AI) is equally important as coffee in the morning, and it's getting easier to obtain.

I'll explain it to you using some examples from real life. Consider Netflix as an example. Do you recall when Netflix rented out DVDs? These days, artificial intelligence anticipates your viewing preferences before you even realize it. That's how such shows manage to keep you captivated. By providing the appropriate content at the perfect moment to keep you interested, AI helped them become a dominant force.

Blockbuster is next up. I assume you remember Blockbuster. They had the option to board the AI train, but they decided against it. They opposed the change, and the world moved on without them, so now they are just a memory.

The truth is that artificial intelligence is a necessity rather than just a neat technology. To achieve success in the next ten years for your business, you must integrate AI into your operations. It's about surviving.

WHY AI IS ESSENTIAL FOR BUSINESS SUCCESS

Okay, let's get right in and see why artificial intelligence is your new best friend in business. AI, for starters, doesn't sleep. It doesn't require a coffee break, doesn't take time off for vacation or call in sick, and never ends the workday. It increases the efficiency of every single facet of your business or organization.

Consider the marketing domain. Do you recall a time when you had to estimate what your consumers wanted? While many of us conducted occasional surveys and market research, it was essentially a guessing game. AI eliminates the need for guesswork. With AI-powered solutions, you may obtain data-driven insights instantly. By launching a precise missile that consistently hits the objective, you're not just hurling objects at the wall to see what sticks.

How about the operations? AI has that covered, too. It can optimize supply chains by automating routine daily tasks. AI removes everything's productivity. Customer service comes next. AI can do routine tasks like responding to FAQs and freeing up your human representatives to handle more complicated problems that require human intervention. It resembles having a world-class squad that never skips a day of play.

Let's discuss money. Fintech is where AI truly starts to shine. Imagine having perfect accuracy when predicting financial trends. We are discussing how to make choices based on information so accurate that it resembles a crystal ball. AI can spot trends you might miss and warn you of impending threats. It's a significant competitive advantage. In today's fast-paced industry, making quick, data-driven decisions might mean the difference between a terrible failure and a successful end.. Businesses of all sizes, from the neighborhood mom-and-pop store to the expanding Silicon Valley company, can now access AI solutions. Success is becoming more accessible to everyone with the intelligence to use artificial intelligence (AI).

HOW AI IS REVOLUTIONIZING PERSONAL AND BUSINESS CREDIT

Right now, I'm going to discuss with you the reasons behind AI's current status as one of The Great American Credit Secrets. Everyone knows how important it is to have good credit, but how can we increase it without resorting to more conventional means? That is like attempting to carve a statue with a spoon, man. All of a sudden, you're carrying a laser cutter when you enter AI.

Artificial intelligence is automating credit assessments and rewriting the rules. You won't have to wait weeks to receive loan approval. AI is capable of performing financial analysis, estimating creditworthiness, and making decisions more quickly than you can check your email. For small firms, where time equals money, that is revolutionary. We'll go over particular techniques in this book that you may use to manage your business and personal credit portfolio.

However, that is only the start. Moreover, AI customizes credit solutions. It takes more than merely accepting or rejecting loans. AI examines your unique circumstances and modifies the terms to satisfy your business's needs. It's similar to having a credit counselor at your side all the time, ensuring that you're receiving the greatest bargain.

Here are some additional functions that AI performs in the credit industry.

- Credit monitoring
- Fraud Detection
- Risk Management
- Score Boosting

AI is the difference between riding a jet ski to the top of a hill and carrying a backpack full of bricks for businesses attempting to establish their credit score.

To put it briefly, AI is the key to enabling quicker and more effective credit-building techniques. AI is the tool that will help you get there, whether you're a major organization trying to remain ahead of the curve or a small business owner trying to get a leg up. If you don't use Blockbuster, you risk falling behind.

This book will guide you through helpful websites and apps to maximize artificial intelligence. AI is the future of business, and that future is now.

AI is now one of The Great American Credit Secrets.

ONE
GENERATING BUSINESS IDEAS WITH AI

Let's dive into the topic of generating multimillion-dollar ideas using artificial intelligence. Obviously, we understand that spotting the next big deal or unicorn is not always an effortless task. Sometimes it feels as if it's not attainable. But... what if I said there's a way to make this whole thing automated and both faster and smoother? You see, that's where AI steps in. AI and various platforms, such as IdeaNoFutureFinder, have become your new allies.

IDEANOTE: TRANSFORMING BIG DATA INTO BIG IDEAS

Let's begin utilizing the Ideanote platform. This platform functions similarly to a team of geniuses working around the clock, but instead of coffee breaks and brainstorming sessions, they are crunching data. They analyze trends and provide you with innovative ideas and philosophies. You're probably asking yourself, "Can a machine generate ideas as good as those my own team generates?" The quick answer is yes, but the truth is that it can sometimes generate even better ideas. Here's what I truly want you to understand about AI. AI doesn't simply generate random ideas from various sources. It's not like tossing a bunch of words into a hat and then suddenly pulling one out—not at all. Instead, it digs deep into data. It analyzes everything from market trends to consumer behavior and things of that nature. It sifts through massive amounts of information that would normally take a person weeks or even months to process, including various types of research. The best part is that it's in real-time. It provides fresh, up-to-date, minute-by-minute ideas relevant to current events. It focuses on what's relevant right now.

You see, it's not just about throwing ideas out and throwing them there and hoping something eventually hits. Ideanote aligns those AI-generated ideas with your business goals, values, and perspectives. It's like a GPS for innovation. It keeps you on the right path while also suggesting the best route to take. You set the parameters, tweak the settings, and guide the AI to focus on the most important aspects of your business.

In this way, you're not just getting ideas. You're getting all of the right ideas. A prime example of this is someone who works in the fitness industry. If you're a company that's in the fitness space, for example, somebody might come to you and say, "Hey, I'm trying to lose belly fat," so that when you're talking to AI and things like Ideanote, you're going to center it around belly fat, because that's one of the things that come up a lot. Alternatively, other individuals may inquire, "What's a good diet plan?" Simply formulate that around your business, and they'll help you formulate the right ideas. For instance, if you own a fashion brand, the system could analyze the sentiment surrounding eco-friendly products and keep track of the latest trends and materials. It could even predict your target audience for the next season or event. And what's the result of that? It's a list of ideas that's not just innovative but perfectly aligned with your brand's mission. This list is not exclusive to established businesses. If you're attempting to establish a business that will carve out your niche, you want to use Ideanote. This approach can assist you in identifying market gaps. It can help you brainstorm products. It assists you with strategies to differentiate yourself from the competition. It's similar to a crystal ball that shows you where the opportunities are and how to capitalize.

Here's yet another example...

When I started my credit repair business, I knew there were some people in the industry who were also good. To differentiate myself, I thought of unique marketing trends. So, I invented the Giant Credit Card. With the Giant Credit Card, I would go to a restaurant or somewhere and tell the cashier to pretend to ring me up with my Giant Credit Card. While this was taking place, I would have someone film it. This was hilarious—out of the ordinary—but more importantly, it made my brand more memorable. The truth of the matter: It took me some time to come up with that idea. However, if you were to create something akin to an Ideanote or similar, you could simply ask yourself, "What are some unconventional, humorous, and unique ideas that would help me stand out to my audience?" Those are the types of things that you want to incorporate when making your brand and choosing a name. You want to establish your brand as a forward-thinking entity by closely monitoring trends and identifying potential opportunities in the present.

FUTUREFINDER BY TRENDWATCHING: SPOTTING TOMORROW'S OPPORTUNITIES TODAY

If Ideanote serves as your idea factory, then FutureFinder can be compared to a treasure map. This platform identifies emerging markets and untapped opportunities, and it analyzes global trends currently shaping our society. You know, when we talk about looking at the big picture, spotting where the world is headed, and figuring out your business, that's exactly what you need to do. That's how you discover the path to success. So FutureFinder uses AI to analyze a bunch of data from different parts of the world—social media, news articles, research papers, all of the above. It's like a supercharged Trend Hunter. It constantly seeks the next big thing, which is great. The best part is not just telling you what's happening right now; it's also predicting what's going to happen next. Could you imagine being able to spot a trend before it even actually happens? Sheesh! You guys, this is huge!

FutureFinder provides precisely that kind of insight. It's like being able to see into the future and position your business ahead of whatever is to come, whether it's new technology, a shift in consumer behavior, or an emerging market. FutureFinder helps you spot these opportunities early so you can capitalize on them.

Let's look at a real-life example. Let's say you're in the tech industry, and you need to know what's going to be the next big thing for consumers in electronics. They might analyze trends and suggest that wearable tech is poised for significant growth, or they might even identify a specific type of device that consumers are enthusiastic about. With this information, you can begin developing your product line, obtaining patents, or initiating marketing as a business leader, thereby gaining a competitive advantage. You get ahead of the niche.

You've already established yourself before the rest of the industry arrives. And it's not just about products. Future Finder can help you identify shifts in consumer values. You could change norms. You can even find different ways of doing business. For example, during the pandemic, we saw a huge shift toward remote people working remotely. That's why companies like

DocuSign became prevalent, and Zoom became very notable, credible companies. This is because businesses that spotted this trend early were able to pivot, offer remote, friendly services, and thrive in challenging environments. So FutureFinder helps you catch those waves and ride them to success.

ALIGNING AI WITH BUSINESS STRATEGIES

So it's important to remember that while AI is an amazing tool if utilized the right way, it's also not a magic wand; I can't say this enough. You can't just sit back and think you're going to let it do all the work. It doesn't work like that. The real magic happens when you align these AI-generated ideas with your overall strategies in business. So, think of it as a partnership with AI. You know, that's your automated business associate. AI provides the data and insights, and then you offer the vision, strategy, and implementation. Therefore, when utilizing platforms such as Ideanote, Future Finder, and others, it's crucial to have a thorough understanding of your business, its goals, traditions, and values. For example, if you are focusing on sustainability, innovation, and customer experience, make sure your AI-generated ideas match those goals. This way, you're not just chasing trends; you're also building a business that's true to your vision and values.

Remember, one of the things I consistently emphasize is that when you genuinely engage in what you love, you never work a day in your life. My advice is to find a business doing something you already enjoy and are passionate about. Now, it's also crucial to involve your team in the process. While AI can generate ideas, your team is responsible for bringing these ideas to life. So, make sure that you involve your shareholders, your team, your mastermind groups, and your associates. Make sure you engage in collaborative brainstorming, solicit their thoughts and feedback, and ensure that everyone is in agreement.

One of the things I did when I developed Credit Genius was to ask everyone who was involved in the company what their opinions were whenever I made a big change. I also consulted AI, whom I consider a valuable member of my team as well. But I also asked the marketing director and the intern. I reached out to the CTO, the engineers, and everyone involved in the project. Not only will this assist you in generating ideas, but it will also guarantee your team's commitment to successfully launching your project, from conception to implementation, and transforming AI-generated concepts into reality.

Generating ideas with AI is a crucial first step, but the real challenge and opportunities lie in bringing these ideas to life. You have to make those come true. Your leadership, team, execution, motivation, and determination matter here. You begin by assessing the AI-generated ideas, considering their alignment with your goals, the impact they may have, and, above all, your personal passion. After you've nailed down your options, it's time to get to work. So develop a plan to bring these ideas to life. This may entail activities such as product development, market research, securing funding, and prototyping, but it's crucial to establish clear milestones and deadlines and to hold both yourself and your team accountable for meeting them. Remember, AI can generate the idea, but I want to reiterate that it's your responsibility to turn it into reality. It's up to you to make them a reality. So don't be afraid to iterate and pivot as you go. You're going to have to be flexible, stay open to feedback, and keep refining your approach until you master it.

One of the things I always remind people is that while you have the option to write a business plan, it's important to remember that things in business never go 100% as planned. Always be ready for the bumps on the road. While AI-generated ideas rely on data, they don't necessarily remain unchangeable. As you begin to implement, you may discover that certain concepts require modification or adjustment based on insights gained from the process. Be flexible, stay open to feedback, and keep refining your approach until you get it right. One more thing to remember: every once in a blue moon, AI can make an error.

Every now and then, AI is wrong. For the most part, AI will generate great ideas and similar concepts, but it's important to also conduct some due diligence. I recall a time using ChatGPT and asking, "How many Rs are in the word strawberry?" And ChatGPT would come back and say, "Two." The machine correctly counted the second R in "berry," but it failed to count the first R in "straw." This is a brilliant machine, but it occasionally makes small errors. Therefore, it's important to keep track of these errors while you're working on your ideas and to measure your success at the end.

You also want to use analytics and data to track the performance of your AI-generated ideas. You want to find out what's working, what's not working, and what you can use to generate even better ideas in the future. So AI is a tool, but remember that it's also a learning process. Therefore, the more you utilize it, the more proficient you will become in harnessing its potential to propel your business and company forward.

Platforms such as ChatGPT can also take your idea and assist you in formulating the business plan we previously discussed. The goal is to thoroughly explain the chatbot, how you want it to work, and how you plan to make money. You can also consult ChatGPT for ideas or alternative methods to generate revenue for your business. Platforms like this and others are only as useful as the information you give them, so be sure to put in as much information as you possibly can. Another feature of ChatGPT is a microphone button. When you click this button, it records your voice and transcribes it, allowing you to converse with ChatGPT without interruption. Communicate with it as if it were a friend or a business partner, provide it with all the necessary information, and then allow it to transcribe it, providing the data you require for your business and your niche. It's also a good idea to leverage successful businesses that are similar to yours to identify what has worked for them. For example, Credit Genius has a similar business model to Credit Karma. Credit Karma's business model was amazing. That's why they're an $8 billion company.

However, we took their successful practices and incorporated them into our model while excluding the mistakes they made. Remember, if successful methods work for others, there's a good chance they will also work for you.

THE AI-DRIVEN BUSINESS OF TOMORROW

Structuring your business with AI goes beyond following trends. You have to remember it's about positioning yourself for success in an ever-changing world. So by leveraging AI tools like Ideanote and FutureFinder, you're not just generating ideas; you're generating the right ideas. You're not just spotting trends; you're spotting the right ones. You're not just building a business. You're building a business that is poised for the future, right? For sure, without a doubt, 100%, indubitably, AI is a GAME CHANGER. But again, just like any tool, it's only as effective as how you use it. So embrace it. You could leverage it. You could witness its power as it propels your business to unprecedented heights. AI is the future of business, and with the right approach, it looks pretty damn bright. Wouldn't you agree?

Pretty soon we're going to learn how to incorporate all of this with personal and business credit and still use AI to our advantage.

Now that we're beginning to understand these tips, I encourage you to take action and create some amazing results.

TWO
NAMING YOUR BUSINESS WITH AI

Okay, so let's say you have finally found an amazing business idea, and now you're ready to go ahead and take it to the next level. Before you go any further, let's think: What is it that you need? You need a fantastic name, not just any name—a name that pops, a name that sticks, a name that rings—a name that people will remember in their minds, and, trust me, in a crowded marketplace, this is a lot easier said than done. I know from actual experience that this is where AI steps in. I'm going to introduce you to the tools that will make naming your business not only easier, but also enjoyable. The first step is to craft a brand that stands out. Let's go ahead and talk about name licks. Name licks are more than just a name generator. It functions similarly to a personal branding consultant, but it is also powered by AI.

Okay, I know what you're thinking: *Why can't I just brainstorm some names on my own?* The truth is, yes, you can, but why not take advantage of AI's ability to analyze these specific industry keywords, these linguistic patterns, and also the market trends that are associated with something truly special? Name Licks doesn't just spit out random names; it actually generates brandable names that resonate with your target audience.

Let's look at some of the biggest brands out there. You got Nike, you got Tesla, you got Apple. These names did not emerge by chance. Think about it. They're simple, memorable, and say something about the brand's identity. That's precisely what Name Licks strives to accomplish. It takes into account the vibe you want to project, the industry you're interested in, and the kind of impact you want your name to have.

Let's say, for example, that you're starting a tech company that focuses on AI-driven solutions. Okay, you type in some keywords, like AI tech innovation, and Name Licks starts doing what it does best. It will take those keywords, analyze them alongside linguistic trends, and suggest names that not only sound cool but also align with the latest trends. It might suggest names that lack any AI or tech-related connotations. Not only are these names catchy, but their strategic design also resonates with the "super techy" audience you are targeting. Okay, but remember this: it's not just about being catchy. Your brand name has to have staying power. It needs to be something people can remember after hearing it more than once. Here's another thing: Name Licks excels at capturing current trends, but it also has the potential to stand the test of time—that's the sweet spot you're aiming for. You want a name that's not only trendy but also timeless. Ideally, it should work across platforms like Evergreen, Shopify, and be optimized by a business name generator, making your name SEO-friendly and legally sound.

Now let's say, for example, you have a few potential names that are lined up thanks to name licks. What do you want to do next?

You need to make sure your name isn't just unique but also SEO-friendly and legally available. This is where the Shopify Business Name Generator comes in. Okay? This tool enhances your brand name strategy by assisting you in securing a unique and search engine-optimized name. To begin, let's discuss SEO, or search engine optimization. For those who are unfamiliar with SEO, it's important to understand that if your business doesn't appear on Google, it doesn't actually exist. This underscores the importance of having an SEO-friendly name. It's instrumental to success in business. Shopify is a tool that helps you generate names that aren't just catchy, but also likely to rank well in those search engine results. It's about striking that perfect balance between creativity and practicality. For instance, let's imagine that your business idea is an online store that sells eco-friendly products. Do you want a name that reflects your green mission while also hitting those SEO sweet spots? Okay? The Shopify generator may recommend names such as "green goods CO" or "eco essentials," as these names not only emphasize your eco-friendly focus, but also have a specific structure that increases the likelihood of your business ranking higher in search results when people are searching for green products and services.

However, keep in mind that selecting a name such as Shop Online Direct, which is expansive and ambiguous, could potentially obscure your brand amidst the thousands of Google searches already containing this information. This is a key thing to remember. Okay, but wait, there's more exclamation. What about domain name availability? You don't want to fall in love with a name only to discover it's already in use or, even worse, that someone else is already operating under that name. The Shopify Business Name Generator verifies the availability of the generated domain name, ensuring the security of your online presence from the outset. Then let's not forget the legal aspect: you want to make sure your chosen name isn't already a trademark or in use by another company. Therefore, engaging in legal disputes over your business name is not what you desire. Trust me, an AI tool like Shopify Generator is going to help you avoid these pitfalls, and it does so by cross-referencing other trade-marks of existing businesses.

It's like having a legal team on standby, making sure you're in the clear before you go ahead and print up those business cards or lock in that LLC. This underscores the significance of having a robust online presence. Okay, so you've got your name. It's catchy, SEO-friendly, and legally available. Nobody else has it. It's customized for you. It's trendy. This is really just the beginning because in today's world, your business's online presence is everything. Your name, essentially, is a gateway to your brand's digital identity. It's not just about having a website; it's about having the exact right website with the right domain name that's simple to find, simple to remember, or both. AI tools like Shopify Generator ensure that the name you choose translates perfectly across your online presence, regardless of whether it's securing the ".com" domain or making sure your name looks appealing in the logo. All of these tools. Have you covered it? Remember, your business name is often the first interaction that people will have with your brand. It's got to be memorable, catchy, strong, and perfectly aligned with your digital strategy. When you're figuring this out, it's important to incorporate all these elements together. Let's take Amazon as an example. Okay, that name is simple; it's global and instantly recognizable. But in terms of SEO, it's a powerhouse. In terms of domain presence, it's a powerhouse. When you type Amazon into Google, it immediately appears; this is the type of impact you want to aim for. With AI, you can achieve a level of strategic branding that is within your reach.

Lastly, let's focus on the most important aspect. A credibility check is a crucial step in establishing your business and business credit. Often, when you apply for funding, banks will perform a reverse lookup. This means looking at your online presence. If your business is not listed online, then you look like a ghost; like I said before, you don't exist. Therefore, a bank may question your legitimacy if your business isn't listed online. Never ever set yourself up like that. You want to see as many places as possible. That's also why I suggest getting into as many publications, press, YouTube videos, and Amazon as you possibly can.

As more people see and mention you, your credibility increases. Even free apps and social media sites add more credibility to your brand. Then, if you're able, I'll go ahead and attempt to get verified. Many of these social media sites allow you to pay for verification. I understand that we typically don't want to spend an extra $15 a month, but for brand credibility, it's crucial. It could mean the difference between someone copying your idea or deciding to purchase your service, to sum it up. What's the main lesson to be learned from the AI advantage? It's true that naming your business is really no small task. However, thanks to AI tools such as Shopify, naming your business doesn't have to be a daunting task. Business generator. These are your secret weapons. These will help you craft a brand name that's not just memorable but also sounds strategic. These tools will analyze everything from market trends to SEO factors and other things to ensure that your business name is poised for success right out of the gate.

Again, remember, AI is just a tool. It's up to you to take those AI-generated names, make them your own, and formulate them in your own way. You bring the vision, you bring the goals, you bring the passion, and you bring the values.

AI will bring the data. AI will bring the trends. AI will gather the necessary analytics, and when combined, these elements can transform your brand from a mere household idea into a household name. So don't just settle for the name. The first thing that pops into your mind is that you want to leverage AI to explore each and every possibility, to go out and refine all your choices, and to make your business name into one that will stand the test of time.

Remember, it only takes about 30 seconds to generate a search once you input the information, but the quality of the search depends on the quality of the information you provide. After all, your business deserves a name as strong and unique as you, a founder.

So, let's go ahead and make that happen!

THREE
DEFINING YOUR BUSINESS OPERATIONS WITH AI

Now that we've already discussed generating those fantastic business ideas and being able to pinpoint future opportunities utilizing AI, it's time to get down to the nitty-gritty of defining your business operations with some assistance from our tech-savvy friend, Mr. AI!

In this chapter, we're going to go ahead and dive into how artificial intelligence can help you stay ahead of the curve with exploding topics and help you choose the right industry classification to set your business up for long-term success. This is also crucial in the credit world, and you're about to discover why exploding topics remain ahead of the curve.

Let's begin by focusing on one of the most powerful tools in your AI arsenal: Exploding Topics.

Imagine having the ability to know how to blow up in your industry before any other company does. It sounds like a superhuman power, right? Well, that's exactly the kind of thing that AI provides. It's a leg up on the competition by identifying the most relevant industry trends and protocols that are currently happening, not after they have already happened.

Exploring topics feels like a journey to the fourth dimension. This AI-driven tool searches and analyzes vast amounts of data from the internet. This includes social media buzz, search engine queries, and news articles. It essentially identifies trends that are picking up steam. However, this isn't just about finding out what's a hot topic right now. The goal is to predict what will be hot tomorrow, next year, and the year after. So how does this help your business operations? The answer to that is simple. It stays ahead of the trends, allowing you to come in and adapt your operations to meet market demands, not just current ones but also future ones. For example, if you're in the health and wellness industry and an exploding topic shows you that there's growing interest—let's say plant-based supplements—then you can go ahead and use this insight to adjust your product line and bring up production, or even begin your marketing tactics for your existing products before your competitors are any wiser.

It's about being proactive instead of reactive. I often say, "AI can help you." AI will help you beat trends in all areas of your business. For example, new software in your industry may explode, or customer behavior may change, affecting how you deliver your product or service. In either scenario, AI has the ability to detect these changes at an early stage, allowing you to make necessary adjustments and maintain a competitive edge. Use AI-assisted classification tools to obtain your NAICS code immediately.

Let's discuss a topic that may not seem as exciting or controversial, but it's crucial nonetheless: selecting the appropriate industry classification for your business. Specifically, we're talking about the NAICS code, which stands for North American Industry Classification System. Okay, this code might sound like a bunch of mumbo-jumbo technical terms, but trust me, getting this right is huge for your business. Any serious entrepreneur will not skip this step. Why is this? Because your NAICS code isn't just a random number that the government uses to categorize you. It has real-world implications, especially when it comes to things like business.

One of my favorite topics is credit, securing funding, and the perception investors, banks, and lenders have of your business. In other words, this is an essential piece of your business identity. One thing I want you to remember is that the NAICS code is definitely different from your EIN code. Your EIN code acts as a kind of social security number for your business. However, the NAICS code is a number that identifies what type of business you have. Here's the thing you're choosing: the right NAICS code isn't always straightforward. While you may believe your business fits perfectly into one category, AI-assisted industry classification tools may suggest a more advantageous code for you in the long run. These AI tools can analyze your business model. They can compare it with other businesses and suggest the best NAICS code that's also the lowest risk. It's kind of like having a consultant who knows the ins and outs of every industry.

By using AI, you can ensure that the code you choose aligns with your business's operations, positioning you for the highest level of success within your potential industry. Let's start with an example. Let's say you have a tech startup that specializes in AI-driven healthcare solutions. You might be inclined to categorize your business under a general healthcare code, but the use of AI tools may reveal a more specialized code for medical software development, which could potentially lead to increased funding opportunities or enhance your standing in your industry. I'm going to give you another example. Many individuals own real estate companies and aspire to venture into the real estate market, yet most banks perceive real estate as a significant risk factor. Why? A real estate deal requires numerous factors to achieve success. You have to have the right type of buyer. You must choose the right type of seller. If the transaction entails a fix and flip, it's imperative to secure all required materials. Make sure that all zones are clearly defined. Ensure that the property's construction lasts the appropriate amount of time. You need to ensure that the materials used are of the correct type. Real estate and real estate flipping involve numerous variables across different categories. Another NAICS code focuses on property management. Every property requires management in some form or another.

If you present your business as property management or a similar business and use the NAICS code, banks will view it favorably, making you appear more credible and less risky to them. And it doesn't stop there, right? The correct NAICS code could also affect your business credit profile in its entirety; banks, lenders, and investors often look at that when they decide your creditworthiness. More accurate code reflects your business's true nature. It can make you look more credible, as well as financially stable. It can also help you look at industry-specific grants or incentives that you might not otherwise have been eligible for if you have had a different classification. As a credit repair company, we have to be very strategic about how we present ourselves, and a lot of the time, we present ourselves as an educational company, and that's how we set up our operations to educate the general audience. Why is this because of a credit repair company's bank reasons and mostly because of a conflict of interest? Banks view us as a red flag, but if we educate people, they see us as a green light.

ChatGPT and NAICS code selection. Okay, let's bring ChatGPT back into the conversation. Okay, you may have wondered: Can ChatGPT help me choose the right NAICS code? The answer is absolutely. ChatGPT, like other AI tools, could assist you in navigating the complexities of being able to classify your industry. It could give a detailed description of your business activities. ChatGPT can also suggest low-risk NAICS codes that are similar to your industry. This is how it works. You describe your business to ChatGPT. Describe your goals, customers, fears, hopes, and how to achieve them. Remember, I'm repeating what I've already said. It's only as useful as your information; therefore, describe your industry. It will also compare different types of NAICS codes and explain the pros and cons of each, enabling you to make the best-informed decision.

In ChatGPT, you should include the following prompt: Help me decide which ICS code is the lowest risk for my industry. And guess what? The best part about all of this is that you're not alone. You can use ChatGPT as a kind of sounding board. You can ask follow-up questions. You could get more detailed insights. You could refine your selection. It's kind of like an AI-powered business advisor. Again. We talked about this earlier. This is a member of your team. If you're choosing your NAICS code for the first time or reclassifying your business, tools like ChatGPT and others can be a game changer because they eliminate guesswork and give you the confidence to make an informed decision.

This is important for credit because banks want to know what kind of company you are when you apply for funding. Even with excellent credit or business credit, if you raise red flags, the bank may immediately deny your application. And we definitely don't want that for you—the long-term impact of industry classification. I don't want you to forget about the long-term impact of your NAICS code. This isn't just a one-and-done decision; it's something that can affect your business forever.

Therefore, choosing the correct code can lead to new opportunities, enhance your credit profile, and position your business for growth in a fiercely competitive market. It's similar to laying the foundation for your business, just as you wouldn't build a house on unstable or unreliable ground. You wouldn't want your business to fall into a category.

So again, by using AI tools to get the right NAICS code, you are setting yourself up for success right from the start. Remember, as your business evolves, your NAICS code could also evolve. Don't be afraid to revisit this decision as your company grows and expands. AI can assist you in maintaining agility, ensuring that your classification aligns best with your company's scale. One particular thing to keep in mind is that some NAICS codes pose a high risk to banks. One last thing to remember (and I want to repeat): some NAICS codes are high-risk to banks, and some are low-risk, so choose wisely!

CONCLUSION: DEFINING OPERATIONS WITH PRECISION

Breaking down your business operations with AI is more than keeping up with trends or to-dos. It's about positioning your business to achieve long-term success in a world that is always evolving and changing. If you use tools like exploding topics and AI-assisted industry classification, you're not just defining your operations, but you're making them very precise, which is what you want. AI gives you the power and momentum to stay ahead, adapt, meet demands, and be strategic, setting you apart from the competition. It also helps you see the bigger picture, manages your details, and ensures that every aspect of your business aligns perfectly with your goals.

Don't forget to perform these chatGPT searches again. It literally only takes 30 seconds for each search. It's not a very long, drawn-out, tedious process at all, which is its beauty, especially today. In today's society, efficiency is crucial. With that said, don't just settle for doing business as usual. This is 2024; this is the new age. You will fall behind if you don't use AI. If you are using AI, then you have the ability to leave behind your competitors and fly to new heights.

FOUR
COMPETITOR ANALYSIS AND MARKET LANDSCAPE

All right, now it's time to get down to some serious business. This is the kind of business that separates leaders from followers. This pertains to analyzing competitors and comprehending the market landscape, aided by our automated business partner, artificial intelligence. In this chapter, we're going to explore how some of these AI tools, like CB Insights and Trend Hunter, can give you the insights that are necessary to outsmart your competition and get your company footprint solidly stamped in the marketplace. CB Insights is the ultimate competitor analysis tool. Starting with CB Insights is like having a secret weapon to stay ahead of the competition.

Imagine a business that operates like Sherlock Holmes. It digs deep into the data. It distinguishes between different hidden patterns and provides insights that can make or break your strategy. So what does it do? In summary, it provides comprehensive competitor analysis. This includes everything from market share financial assistance to strategic market moves. It's similar to having a backstage pass to your competition's playbook. You understand what's working for them, what isn't, and how they're positioning themselves in the market, which is invaluable. Remember what I mentioned earlier? You aim to replicate the successful strategies of your competitors while eliminating the ineffective ones. Additionally, you aim to incorporate your unique approach that sets you apart from your competitors.

So imagine for a minute that you're managing a fintech startup and figuring out how to compete with some of the bigger players. CB Insights shows you their financials. That highlights their investment. It even tracks their partnerships. With this data, you can refine your own strategy, potentially targeting a niche that they haven't even considered or introducing a service they don't currently offer. Always look for gaps that others may have missed so you can capitalize on them. However, it's more than just looking at competition in isolation.

To identify growing sectors, stagnant sectors, and the next big opportunities, CB Insights provides a broader market view. It kind of allows you to make data-driven decisions and keeps you ahead of the game. That seems to be one of the common themes of this book: staying ahead of the game. The best part is that CB Insights doesn't just throw data and expect you to figure out the rest for yourself. It utilizes AI to analyze the data and present it in a way that is both understandable and actionable. To understand this, you do not need to be a high-tech data scientist. CB Insights does all the heavy lifting so you can focus on what really matters: making the best decisions for your company.

Say, for example, you discover through CB Insights that one of your competitors is going to launch a new product. There are only really two options. You could react later or use that insight to move forward. You can also ramp up your own product development, or you could adjust your marketing strategy to pinpoint features that their new product hasn't incorporated yet. Either way, you're not just sitting back and watching them run your competition—your entire industry. You're proactive while still remaining competitive. As a trend hunter, you anticipate trends and closely monitor your competitors. So, switch gears.

Let's talk about Trend Hunter. Here's another AI-driven asset that is going to keep you in the loop. It's happening. If CB Insights acts as a detective for you, Trend Hunter resembles a crystal ball. It will help you predict industry trends. It will also assist you in closely monitoring the actions and inactions of your competitors. Trend Hunter uses AI to monitor the market on a continuous basis. It tracks emerging trends and analyzes how they might be impacting your industry. AI-driven technology functions as a trend spotter on your team, continuously providing you with insights into current trends and fads. Doing these things in real time always keeps you up to date. Now here's where it gets interesting. Trend Hunter doesn't just tell you what's happening. It actually tells you what is going to happen. After analyzing data patterns, it predicts market direction and specific trends. This foresight can be game-changing for companies looking to get ahead.

Imagine you're in the fashion industry, and Trend Hunter identifies a growing interest in different sustainable materials. You could potentially use this insight to start sourcing eco-friendly fabrics or adding sustainable products to your repertoire. And by the time your competitors catch on, you've already established yourself as a leader in this train, giving you a significant advantage.

I want to give you a personal example. When I became a public figure with my own brand, I wanted to know how to stand out in credit. What types of things can I do that are different from what other people in the credit field are not doing? I've already demonstrated the significance of the credit card. Another common mistake people make, however, is failing to identify their clients' goals when signing them up for credit repair services. Therefore, when clients sign up for credit repair, they have a specific goal in mind. One person could be trying to buy a house. Another person could be trying to get some credit cards. Another person could be trying to buy a new car. Using parameters similar to CB Insights and Trend Hunter, we identified a list of various items that clients are interested in purchasing with credit, which we then displayed on our website. So when clients see these things on the website, they automatically resonate and say, Hey, these are the things that I want. In a sense, it was working back-ward, but it was utilizing the same trends that Trend Hunter offers to stay ahead of the competition.

But it's not just about predicting trends in itself. Trend Hunter also keeps a close watch on your competitors. It analyzes their movements and provides insights to help you refine some of your own strategies. So, for example, if a competitor shifts their focus to a brand new market, Trend Hunter can alert you of that change. This will give you an opportunity to respond accordingly. Perhaps you choose to remain passive and take no action, or perhaps you seize the opportunity to expand into a new market before they fully establish themselves. Either way, you're not just reacting; you're strategizing, which is instrumental in this world. Don't overlook the role of AI in this process, as Trend Hunter employs AI-advanced algorithms to analyze vast volumes of data. They identify patterns and trends that a human being could potentially miss. This means you're getting insights that are not just accurate but also extremely relevant. You're not relying on your gut instinct or your own guesswork. Some of these things may not be visible to the naked eye. Instead, you're making decisions based on cold, concrete facts, aka concrete data, using AI insights to pivot and enhance market position.

Since we have already covered CB Insights and Trend Hunter, we know that they can help you monitor your competitors and predict trends. Now, how do we use these insights to pivot or enhance your market position? This is where the rubber meets the road, so to speak, because you turn your data into action. AI-driven tools provide significant benefits, including the flexibility to adapt quickly. Therefore, if a new trend emerges or a competitor makes strategic moves in your market, you can quickly adjust your own strategy accordingly. You will want to do this in real time. Agility is crucial, especially in today's fast-paced environment, where adaptability differentiates between failure and success.

Here's another example. Suppose you're in tech, and Trend Hunter identifies a group interest in a particular type of software or a different type of hardware. You could pivot your development resources to focus here, ensuring that you're ready to meet the demand as it increases. Or, for example, if CB Insights shows that a competitor is gaining a share of the market by offering a feature that you do not yet have, then you could go ahead and utilize that feature and add it to your own product line. You see, the key is to use these insights to stay ahead of the competition. You never want to be in a position where you're playing catch-up.

Remember this: it's not just about reacting; it's also about being proactive. If you constantly monitor the market and your competitors, you can spot opportunities to boost your market position. There could be a different niche that's underserved, or maybe there's a way to differentiate your product that nobody else has. Again, AI-driven tools such as CB Insights and Trend Hunter will provide you with the information you need to capitalize on these opportunities. And let's be real: business is all about staying competitive and ahead of the game. It doesn't matter if you're a startup trying to break into an already robust market or if you are an established, older company just trying to stay in the lead. All these situations require the ability to outmaneuver your competition, which AI provides. It provides you with the insights and data you need to make informed decisions and stay ahead of the game—the AI-driven competitive edge.

At the end of the day, competitor analysis and understanding your market are all about gaining a competitive edge. AI provides the edge in today's business world, and as I've repeatedly stated, if you don't utilize it, you risk falling behind. If you master it, then you will be steps ahead of the competition. Many individuals will refrain from utilizing AI. Many individuals will join the AI bandwagon later than others, allowing you to gain a significant competitive advantage. All you need to do is keep training yourself, utilizing these tools, and familiarizing yourself with them. Tools such as CB Insights and Trend Hunter provide you with the necessary insights to stay ahead, enabling you to predict industry trends and make strategic decisions that will secure your position as the first-place gold medal winner.

Again, AI is just a tool. It's how you use it that matters. I emphasize this repeatedly because I genuinely want you to grasp its significance. But if you leverage the power of AI-driven insights, you could refine your strategies. You could pivot when necessary. You can enhance your market position in ways that would be almost impossible without this technology. If not impossible, then it will take a decade to fully learn and enhance these methods. So please don't just sit back as the market changes around you. Go ahead and utilize AI to stay ahead of the game. Outperform your competitors and build a business that's not just surviving but flourishing. The future of business is competitive. With AI on your side, you will be in leading the way.

FIVE
ESTABLISHING YOUR WEB AND ONLINE PRESENCE

Okay, we're on a roll, guys. Now we're going to jump into something absolutely critical in the world of business: your online presence, regardless of whether you're selling products, offering services, or building your brand. Consider that your website is one of your audience's first communications. People research you, your brand, or your company between four and seven times before making a buying decision. Many of these times, they'll go directly to your website. It's like the first stop. It's your digital storefront, right? It's your business card, it's your pitch, it's everything combined. AI is here to ensure that your online presence is not just good but exceptional. In this chapter, we will dive deeply into a variety of AI tools.

You can establish a powerful, professional, and effective online presence with tools such as Wix ADI, Bookmark AiDA, Firedrop List, and Yext. Wix ADI uses artificial intelligence to craft a professional website. Let's begin with Wix ADI, which utilizes artificial design intelligence. If you've ever built a website from scratch, you know that it can be a long, drawn-out task. The template is there. You want to make it customizable. You want to make it reflect your brand. You want to ensure it doesn't look just like all the rest of them. This is exactly where Wix ADI steps in. And I have to say is, this is definitely a game-changer.

WIX ADI

Wix ADI takes the guesswork out of web design instead of spending countless hours trying to figure this thing out, trying to figure out the perfect color scheme and layout, etc. Instead, you can delegate all the work to me. This tool will utilize artificial intelligence (AI) to create a professional, visually appealing website that perfectly aligns with your business. After analyzing your business type, goals, preferences, and other factors, it creates an attractive, brand-aligned website. It analyzes your business, type, goals, preferences, and all that useful stuff and generates a website that doesn't just look useful but is also in alignment with your brand. And that's not it. ADI, or Wix, is more than just its aesthetics. It's essentially about the performance. The AI will optimize your websites based on user experience, UX, and conversion rates. This implies that it considers your visitors' navigation, employs various elements to capture their attention, and guides them toward taking action, such as making a purchase, signing up for a newsletter, or simply contacting you for more information.

Here's an example. Let's say you're running an online store. Wix ADI will design your product pages to present your items optimally. It will ensure that your checkout process is intuitive and smooth so that people will not abandon the cart. So if you're a service provider, Wix ADI will focus on highlighting your offerings, making it simple for potential clients to understand exactly what you do and how to contact you again.

Here's the best part. Wix ADI has the ability to learn and adapt. As your business grows and your needs evolve, your website should evolve too. The AI will continuously analyze user behavior. The AI will make adjustments to enhance the overall user experience. This dynamic approach guarantees the effectiveness and relevance of your website, allowing it to adapt to changing trends and consumer expectations, utilize AI, and streamline the web design process.

BOOKMARK AIDA

Here's another AI power tool that's making waves in the web design world. This is called Bookmark AiDA. So if Wix is about crafting a beautiful, high-performing website, Bookmark AiDA is about doing it quickly and efficiently. AiDA stands for Artificial Intelligence Design Assistant; true to its name, it is here to help you create a magnificent website without all of the hassles and complexities. As an entrepreneur, we know that your time is valuable. You will have a multitude of responsibilities, including product development, marketing, finance, and even finding time for sleep. Ideally, the last thing you should focus on is web design. So that's where Bookmark AiDA shines. It'll automate everything, so you can focus on bookmarking and running your business. You don't need to be a tech wizard or possess advanced knowledge to create a professional website; the AI will ask you basic questions about your business, such as what industry you operate in. What features are important to you? The process will commence in a matter of minutes, during which AiDA will create a fully functional mobile and responsive website. After that's done, you will be ready to go live whenever you see fit. Speaking of mobile responsiveness, we can't overlook how critical it is in today's digital landscape; over half of all web traffic now comes from mobile devices. Your website must look and work well on smartphones, tablets, and desktops.

Bookmark AiDA guarantees your site's optimization for various devices, enabling it to automatically modify layouts, images, and content, resulting in a consistent user experience across all platforms. Remember, automation doesn't mean compromise. AiDA allows for customization. You can easily tweak specific elements. The AI is intelligent, but it's also flexible, which gives you the best of both worlds: part speed and part control, Firedrop, dynamic web design, and an AI assistant.

FIREDROP

Next, let's dive into Firedrop, which is a web design tool that introduces a unique concept. It's an AI assistant named Sasha. So if you're imagining a little robot sitting at the desk typing away, you're not too far off. Sasha is conversational Ai. It will interact with you dynamically in real time. The website is user-friendly and customized to meet your specific business needs. Firedrop's magic lies in its simplicity. You don't need to know anything about coding, designs, or anything of that nature. Instead, simply engage in a conversation with Sasha and explain your vision, and Sasha will bring it to life. Whether you need a sleek portfolio site, an e-commerce platform, or a blog, Sasha is here to guide you through the process. It's going to ask you the right questions, and it's going to offer suggestions along the way.

The difference between Firedrop and others is that it's focused on creating websites that aren't just static pages. Firedrop focuses on developing dynamic platforms that adapt to the growth and changes of your business. Say, for example, you start a small consulting firm, and over time, you expand and add new team members. Let's say you do a podcast. Sasha will help you adapt your website to reflect these changes, and it will continue to meet your needs as your business evolves. Adaptability is crucial here, especially in today's fast-paced business environment. This is because you're not just building a website for today; you're building it for tomorrow, next year, 10 years from now, and beyond.

With AI-driven design, you can feel confident that your site will remain relevant and effective, and it doesn't matter how your business changes.

LISTYOURSELF.NET

Next is List Yourself. Easy online presence management. Having a great website is one thing, but making sure people can find it is quite another thing. This is where tools like List Yourself come into play. List Yourself as your online directory manager. It's simple to list your business across multiple platforms, ensuring that you're visible wherever potential customers may be looking. Here's why it matters. When people search for businesses like yours, they don't just use Google. They also consult local directories, social media platforms, and your website. Industry-specific websites. If you don't have your business listed here, you're losing out on potential customers. Listing yourself ensures coverage across multiple platforms by automatically submitting your business details to numerous directories. However, it's not just about listing. It's also about being consistent. Okay, one of the challenges of managing your online presence is ensuring your business information is accurate and up-to-date across all platforms. List Yourself makes this simple by syncing information across the board, so you don't have to worry about outdated addresses, phone numbers, hours of operation, or unexpected places.

Here's something else that's crucial to remember. Banks do a reverse lookup. It's a part of their credibility. They will verify this after reviewing your personal credit report. After reviewing your business credit, they will verify that the company is legitimate. We've spoken about this before. List Yourself allows the bank to look online and to see that you are an actual operational company. Next expanding. Your online footprint.

YEXT

Now, we're going to jump into Yext. Here's another powerful tool for managing your online presence. Yext goes beyond just listing your business. It helps you control your entire digital footprint. This could include search engines or social media sites. This could be a search engine or social media site. Yext ensures that your business information is accurate, consistent, and available everywhere that matters. One of the standout features of Yext is reverse lookup functionality. This might sound kind of technical, but it's actually pretty straightforward. Banks, lenders, and other organizations use "reverse lookup" as a method to verify your businesses. They'll search for your business online to verify its legitimacy and see if it matches up across different platforms. If there are discrepancies, such as addresses or phone numbers, it could raise red flags and hurt your chances of securing funding. Yext will help you avoid this by keeping your business information consistent and up-to-date across the web. Remember, it's not just about listing your business. It's about managing your reputation and ensuring that your online presence reflects the professionalism and reliability that go with your brand. Here's another benefit of Yext: it has the ability to monitor and respond to customer reviews across multiple platforms.

In today's world, we all know that reviews can make or break a business. Positive reviews can boost your credibility hugely, while negative ones can drive customers to one of your competitors. With Yext, you can stay on top of your reviews. You can respond promptly and professionally to different feedback. Here's the kicker: Yext's AI-driven insights can help you identify trends in your reviews, giving a better understanding of what your customers love and things that you may need to improve on.

This kind of feedback is invaluable as you refine your business operations and as you scale. Conclusion? Building a robust online presence with AI, locking in your web and online presence is no longer an option, folks—it's is a necessity. We live in a world where consumers are constantly connected. Your website and footprint often serve as the first impression, and it's important to remember that there's no second chance to make a first impression. Therefore, AI tools like Wix ADI, Bookmark AiDA, Firedrop, List Yourself, and Yext are revolutionizing the way businesses create and manage their online presence. These tools simplify the intricate aspects of web design. They automate time-consuming processes and ensure that your business is visible, consistent, and competitive in the digital space. It also helps when you're going to fund with credit and a bank is doing a reverse lookup.

Remember, AI is not just a tool; it's a replacement for your own unique vision and strategies. You want to use these tools to amplify your brand, streamline your operations, and enhance the customer experience with AI on your team. Remember, it's not just a website. This is a dynamic, adaptable, powerful online presence that's going to be the foundation for your business's success in this digital age. Don't settle for a mediocre online presence. Leverage the power of AI to create something magnificent that reflects your brand's essence and connects your audience on a deeper level. The future of business is digital, and with the right tools, you are more than ready to take it on.

SIX
MASTERING SEO AND ONLINE BRANDING WITH AI

As businesses continue to change in the digital era, having a strong online presence is important. Search engine optimization (SEO) and strategic online branding are important since it takes more than just being present online to succeed. The purpose of this chapter is to examine how AI-powered solutions can improve your search engine optimization (SEO) efforts, increase brand awareness, and eventually assist your personal and business credit.

Understanding the relationship between SEO and your credit profile will help you leverage AI's potential and develop a comprehensive web strategy that boosts traffic and establishes your credibility with lenders, investors, clients, and vendors.

LOOKA: BUILDING A STRONG VISUAL BRAND IDENTITY FOR SEO SUCCESS

Let's start with Looka, an AI-powered tool that helps you develop a visually consistent brand identity. Though the relationship between branding and SEO may not appear obvious at first, it is actually rather important. Search engines like Google consider a variety of criteria when determining rankings. The visual coherence of your brand significantly influences the overall user experience on websites.

ENHANCING SEO THROUGH VISUAL CONSISTENCY

Establishing trust with your audience is one of the many benefits of having a strong visual identity for your company. Brand familiarity and confidence encourage users to interact with your content, stay on your website longer, and return. These actions will increase your ranking over time because they provide search engines with positive signals.

Looka makes it easier to create comprehensive brand kits, color schemes, and logos. Make sure that your brand is the same on every digital platform. It's important to manage your marketing materials, social media accounts, and website. This continuity helps in developing an understanding of the brand. Moreover, the more identifiable your brand is, the more likely it is that consumers will look for it directly, making increasing organic traffic an essential component of SEO.

Additionally, a well-thought-out, aesthetically pleasing website lowers bounce rates—the proportion of visitors that depart after only seeing one page. A lower bounce rate results in better rankings, indicating to search engines that your website is interesting and relevant. Looka's ability to assist you in designing optimal photos with relevant alt text, descriptions, and file naming conventions further improves your website's SEO by enhancing its performance in image search results.

SEO STRATEGIES FOR BUSINESS GROWTH AND CREDIT ENHANCEMENT

Now that we've established the significance of a strong visual brand identity, let's examine **8 SEO Strategies** that might improve the performance, expansion, and even credit profile of your company. When correctly implemented, the following tactics will help you establish a better, more reputable online presence, as well as improve your online exposure:

1. Keyword Research

Identifying the appropriate keywords is essential to any SEO strategy that works. To identify keywords that are pertinent to your company, use tools such as Ahrefs, SEMrush, or Google Keyword Planner. To contextualize and target certain user intents, concentrate on phrases with high search traffic and low competition. Don't forget to include long-tail and LSI (Latent Semantic Indexing) keywords.

For example, if your company offers credit repair services, you can increase targeted traffic to your website by using phrases like "best credit repair companies" or "how to fix my credit score." Your chances of appearing higher in search results grow when you optimize your content around these keywords.

2. On-Page Optimization

On-page SEO optimizes your website's elements to help it rank higher in search results. This involves producing attention-grabbing title tags, succinct meta descriptions, organizing your content with header tags, and optimizing your URLs with lots of keywords.

For example, the title tag for a well-organized page on "Improving Your Credit Score" should be "Top Strategies to Improve Your Credit Score." The title tag should include the word "Quickly," an H1 tag that summarizes the primary subject, and pertinent H2 and H3 tags to delineate supporting themes. Appropriate internal linking to other relevant pages on your website can also improve the user experience and allow search engines to better crawl your content.

3. Content Strategy
When it comes to SEO, high-quality content is king. Concentrate on producing in-depth, insightful material that addresses your audience's issues and questions. Although longer, more in-depth articles are more likely to score highly, quality should always come first.

For example, a thorough book on getting an 800 credit score might provide tools to help users track their progress, typical problems, and practical advice. Multimedia components like movies and infographics can boost user engagement even further and help your content rank higher in search results.

4. Technical SEO
Technical SEO makes sure that search engines can simply crawl and index your website. Mobile optimization and improvement are important components. Boost page speed, use a robots.txt file to direct search engine crawlers, protect your website using HTTPS, and establish an XML sitemap.

In addition to enhancing user experience, a mobile-friendly, quick-loading, and secure website helps enhance search engine rankings. You may find and address technical problems that might be impeding the functionality of your website with the aid of tools like Google's Mobile-Friendly Test and PageSpeed Insights.

5. Off-Page Optimization

Off-page SEO focuses on off-website actions that impact your search engine rankings. Important components of offline marketing include interacting with social media, acquiring brand mentions, constructing high-quality backlinks from reputable websites, and page enhancement.

One way to increase the authority and traffic to your website is to write a guest post on a respectable finance blog and include a link back to your site. In comparison, posting your material on social media can increase exposure and inspire others to link to your website, which will improve SEO even more.

6. Local SEO

Local SEO is important for businesses that serve a particular location. Include local keywords in your Google My Business listing and make it more optimized. Ensure that your company's data is consistent across regional directories and platforms.

Integrating phrases such as "Miami Credit Counseling Services" into your website if you provide credit counseling in Miami, for instance. For your business to perform well in local search results, your name, address, and phone number (NAP) must be consistent across all platforms.

7. Analytics and Continuous Improvement

SEO calls for ongoing monitoring and adjustment; it is not a one-time effort. Use tools like Google Analytics to monitor your website's effectiveness, perform A/B testing to improve features like CTAs, and rack your keyword ranks with Ahrefs and SEMrush, among other tools. Adding more value to the content or speeding up the page's load time could increase visitor retention and boost SEO results.

8. User Experience (UX)

In SEO, user experience is very important. Ensure that the material on your website is easily readable, the navigation is user-friendly, and the call to action is compelling. A well-designed website not only keeps users interested, but it also sends signals to search engines indicating your website's value and relevance.

A clean, user-friendly website that helps visitors through the process of raising their credit score, for example, is likely to increase site visits, decrease bounce rates, and improve search engine results.

INTEGRATING SEO INTO YOUR BUSINESS CREDIT STRATEGY

Now that we discussed the fundamentals of SEO, let's examine the relationship between SEO and your company's credit. Effective SEO combined with a solid web presence can greatly increase your company's credibility, which is important for investors and lenders to consider when determining your trustworthiness. Here are some different strategies:

1. Building Credibility Through SEO: A well-designed visual brand identity and an optimized website indicate to lenders and investors that your company is reliable, reputable, and well-established. This could positively influence their perception of your company's stability and dependability.

2. Attracting More Customers and Revenue: A higher search engine ranking leads to more visitors, greater visibility, and ultimately more sales. A steady stream of clients and income contributes to a better financial profile, which is essential for preserving and improving your company's credit.

3. Supporting Personal Credit with Business Success: If your company's finances and your personal credit are intertwined, having a profitable company with excellent SEO can assist you in all aspects of your finances. The extra money and stability that SEO generates can make paying off personal debt, lowering credit utilization, and improving your credit rating easier.

4. Preparing for Funding Opportunities: When applying for business, a strong web presence may be a critical factor in terms of funding or credit. Lenders frequently conduct internet research on your company to determine its viability. Your chances of getting favorable lending terms increase with a well-optimized website that has a consistent, clear brand message.

CONCLUSION: THE POWER OF AI IN SEO AND BUSINESS CREDIT

SEO is more than just a technique to achieve greater visibility online in today's digital age; it's a key component of your business plan that affects everything from credit and financing to your whole approach to business operations. You can improve your company's reputation, draw in more clients, and strengthen your credit profile by using AI-driven tools like Looka to create a powerful visual brand identity and implement successful SEO tactics.

To thrive in business, integrating smart SEO into comprehensive company strategies is essential. By leveraging AI and continuously refining your approach, you can ensure your business not only excels online but also builds and maintains a strong reputation with lenders, investors, and clients.

SEVEN
ENHANCING GOOGLE PRESENCE AND BANK VISIBILITY

It's important to have a strong online presence in today's fast-paced digital world. Having a strong online presence is crucial, not just a luxury. It's important to be visible on Google and other platforms, whether your goal is to draw in clients, get bank funding, or gain trust from investors. But being visible isn't as vital as making sure your company's depiction fosters confidence and trust.

This chapter will examine the ways in which AI-powered solutions such as LegalZoom, Bizplan, and ChatGPT can assist you in achieving that. With the ultimate goal of making sure that your company is not only visible but also appreciated by financial institutions, we'll go into the significance of online business registration, writing a strong business plan, and even choosing the appropriate NAICS code to minimize risk.

LEGALZOOM: SECURING YOUR ONLINE BUSINESS REGISTRATION

First up, let's talk about LegalZoom, a major player in the field of online business registration. You may be asking yourself, "Why is registering my business online such a big deal?" at this point. The first step in establishing credibility and making sure your company appears when prospective clients or banks search for you in the digital era is to have your business legally registered and listed online.

Getting your business listed on Google and other platforms is now easier than ever, thanks to LegalZoom's use of AI to automate the business registration process. However, this goes beyond simply checking a box; it involves building a foundation that will sustain your whole online presence. Registering and listing your company in several directories informs search engines that it is a reputable and authentic entity. Consequently, this can raise your search engine ranks and facilitate client discovery.

The advantages don't end there, either. Your great internet presence significantly influences the bank's perception of your company. One of the first things a bank will do when you apply for a loan or credit line is search for you online. They will confirm your company's listing and its consistent display across platforms. If your company is difficult to find or has contradicting information online, it could negatively impact your chances of attracting investment.

Herein lies the strength of LegalZoom. LegalZoom ensures your company's proper registration and listing, enhancing your reputation with clients and lenders. The AI-powered software guides you through the registration procedure, ensuring the avoidance of common errors and the accurate listing of your company in all relevant directories.

LegalZoom offers additional services that could potentially enhance your online presence. They may assist you with obtaining a domain name, setting up a business email account, and even building a basic website, all of which enhance your internet presence. Banks and investors are more likely to regard you favorably if your web presence is more extensive and professional.

However, it goes beyond the present moment. Proper listing and registration are essential components that will help your business expand over time. Having a strong web presence will be essential when you grow into new markets, introduce new goods, or look for more finance. LegalZoom's AI-powered platform simplifies the process of starting, making it an investment in your company's future.

BIZPLAN: CRAFTING A BUSINESS PLAN WITH AI

Once you've registered and listed your company, let's proceed to the next essential element of building a strong online presence: your business strategy. A strong business plan is a living, breathing document that directs the expansion and development of your company. It is not merely a document you write once and then forget about. Your online presence is a key element of that strategy in the current digital era.

Bizplan is an AI-powered tool designed to assist you in creating a comprehensive business plan that showcases your online presence and maintains a professional style. It is more crucial than ever to emphasize this point in your business plan because banks and investors are taking a closer look at a company's digital presence as part of their due diligence process.

By assisting you at every stage of the procedure, Bizplan removes all uncertainty from business planning. Whether you're creating a new plan or honing an old one, Bizplan's AI tools assist you in producing a document that clearly conveys your vision, strategy, and potential while also looking amazing. However, Bizplan differs from other plans because it places a strong emphasis on incorporating your web presence.

Bizplan, for example, assists you in outlining the ways in

which your website, social media accounts, and online marketing initiatives support your broader business plan. This includes information on how you plan to increase website traffic, convert visitors into customers, and cultivate brand loyalty through regular online interaction. Based on industry standards and your present performance, AI tools can even assist you in establishing reasonable targets for online growth.

While your plans are important, how you communicate them is too. You can generate eye-catching graphs, charts, and other visual aids with Bizplan to help you present a compelling web strategy. This is especially crucial when you're showing your business strategy to investors or banks. It is critical that they recognize not only the importance of having an online presence, but also the existence of a well-defined, data-driven strategy for utilizing it to achieve your business objectives.

You should not overlook the financial aspect of things. With Bizplan's AI technologies, you can also project the effects of your online presence on your earnings, costs, and profitability. Bizplan can help you estimate the return on investment and demonstrate how SEO and internet advertising would benefit your bottom line. It takes this level of in-depth financial forecasting to persuade banks and investors that your company is a wise investment.

Furthermore, the process doesn't end once you've written your company plan. Using Bizplan's AI-driven platform, updating and improving your plan as your company develops is simple. This is important because, in today's rapidly evolving digital landscape, a static business plan quickly becomes antiquated. Maintaining your plan up to date guarantees that it will continue to be an important resource for obtaining capital and directing your company's expansion.

USING CHATGPT TO FIND A LOW-RISK NAICS CODE

Now, let's discuss selecting the right NAICS code, a more technical but no less significant step in guaranteeing your company's web presence and bank visibility. Federal agencies categorize enterprises using the NAICS code (I mentioned earlier) in order to gather, examine, and disseminate statistical data. But your NAICS code can also affect your company's creditworthiness and investors' and banks' risk tolerance.

Selecting the appropriate NAICS code can be challenging, particularly if your company operates in more than one industry or doesn't cleanly fall into a predetermined category. Here's when ChatGPT becomes useful. Using artificial intelligence, ChatGPT can assist you in determining the NAICS code that most accurately describes your company while reducing perceived risk.

This is how it operates: You begin by giving ChatGPT a thorough overview of your company, including your target market, your line of business, and the goods and services you provide. Afterward, ChatGPT compares this data to all available NAICS codes to determine which ones are most relevant to your company. Not only that, but ChatGPT also takes into account market trends, industry risk, and even the potential effects of different codes on your eligibility for specific grants, loans, or tax advantages.

Let's take an example: your company is in the technology industry, but you also do research and development. Depending on your classification, your company might receive a higher-risk NAICS code, which could complicate funding or result in higher loan interest rates. Using ChatGPT, you can investigate more risk-averse option codes that still accurately identify your company.

This is about being strategic, not just about playing it safe. Businesses with a higher-risk classification may not be able to access government contracts, funding opportunities, and other resources unless they have the appropriate NAICS code. Finding a low-risk NAICS code with ChatGPT can set up your company for long-term success.

Consistency holds significant importance. It's crucial to utilize your chosen NAICS code consistently in all of your business papers, such as your business plan, tax filings, and registration. This consistency can boost your credibility and increase your chances of getting finance by helping to solidify your company's identity and making it simpler for banks and investors to comprehend what you do.

INTEGRATING AI TOOLS INTO YOUR OVERALL STRATEGY

After discussing how LegalZoom, Bizplan, and ChatGPT may improve your bank's visibility online, let's discuss how to incorporate these tools into your overall business plan. Recall that the objective is to develop a unified, comprehensive strategy that makes use of AI to establish a solid, trustworthy online presence that appeals to financial institutions as well as consumers.

Use LegalZoom to ensure the correct registration and listing of your company online. This forms the basis of your internet presence and is essential to establishing trustworthiness with banks, consumers, and search engines. To further improve your online presence, make sure all of the information about your company is consistent across all platforms and make use of LegalZoom's other services, such as website construction and domain registration.

Next, build a thorough business strategy that emphasizes your internet presence using Bizplan. Stress the connection between your digital strategy and your overarching business objectives. You can use Bizplan's AI technologies to create visually appealing financial predictions and graphics that will captivate banks and investors. Your business plan should reflect any modifications to your internet approach or business model.

Lastly, use ChatGPT to select a low-risk NAICS code that minimizes perceived risk and accurately describes your company. This calculated move can raise your credit score, provide access to capital, and strengthen the long-term survival of your company. To strengthen your company's identification and legitimacy, consistently use the NAICS code in all of your business papers.

Incorporating these AI tools into your plan helps you establish a solid, trustworthy online presence that banks and investors can rely on, in addition to making sure your company is visible online. As a result, obtaining capital, expanding your company, and reaching your long-term objectives will all be simpler.

CONCLUSION: BUILDING A FUTURE-PROOF BUSINESS WITH AI

In the current digital era, it is more crucial than ever to make sure your company is visible to banks and investors and has a favorable web presence. But being strategic is just as important as being present. LegalZoom, Bizplan, and ChatGPT are just a few examples of AI tools that you can use to build a solid, comprehensive web presence that can improve your business's bank visibility and creditworthiness.

LegalZoom ensures your company's correct registration and online listing, assisting you in laying the foundation. With Bizplan, you can create a detailed business plan that highlights your internet strategy and appeals to investors. Additionally, ChatGPT assists you in choosing the appropriate NAICS code to reduce risk and set up your company for success.

But keep in mind that these are only instruments. It is your responsibility to make good use of them and integrate them into a strategy that will support your company's expansion and long-term success. You're creating a firm that is future-proof and prepared to flourish in an increasingly digital environment, not just an online presence.

Utilize AI's capabilities to make sure that banks, investors, and clients alike view your company as legitimate and respectable in addition to being noticeable. You're more than ready to take on the digital business world of the future if you have the correct plan in place.

EIGHT
UNDERSTANDING BUSINESS CREDIT SCORES

Credit ratings are important in business finance because they influence a company's ability to obtain cash, the conditions of that access, and even the quality of its relationships with vendors and suppliers. This chapter offers a thorough analysis of the several company credit ratings that can affect these variables, emphasizing the elements that go into calculating each score, what it means, and how it affects banking and financial choices.

1. Small Business Scoring Service (SBSS)

The term "Small Business Scoring Service," or SBSS for short, refers to a credit scoring technique that is frequently used by lenders, especially the Small Business Administration (SBA), to assess a company's creditworthiness. Combining the financial information of the company with its credit history and the personal credit histories of the business owner(s) results in a score that offers a comprehensive assessment.

Score Range: A SBSS score ranges between 0 and 300. SBA-backed loans often demand a score of 140 or higher, while certain lenders can have higher requirements.

Components:
• **Business Credit Data:** Incorporates payment history, credit utilization, and public records (like bankruptcies).
• **Personal Credit Data:** The score also takes into account the personal credit history of the business owner(s), as small firms sometimes have financial ties to their owners.
• **Business Financials:** Financial information such as revenue, assets, and liabilities.

Uses:
• **Loan Approval:** The SBSS score is one of the first requirements in loan approval processes, especially for SBA loans.
• **Credit Decisions**: Beyond SBA loans, other financial institutions use the SBSS score for credit choices, such as issuing lines of credit or business credit cards.

Importance:
• **Faster Loan Decisions:** The SBSS approach expedites loan decisions, thereby reducing time and paperwork.
• **Broad Consideration:** By factoring in both business and personal credit data, the score provides a comprehensive perspective.

Small business owners need a high SBSS score to secure funding, especially when applying for SBA-supported loans or other forms of credit.

2. Paydex Score

Overview: Dun & Bradstreet (D&B) gives the Paydex score, which is a different credit score that focuses on a company's past payments to its vendors and suppliers. It's a crucial indicator that lenders, suppliers, and other creditors use to determine how creditworthy a company is.

Score Range: The Paydex score is a number between 0 and 100.

80 or Above: Indicates prompt or early payments.

50 to 79: Payments are typically made within 30 days of the due date.

49 or Below: Payments are frequently overdue by more than 30 days.

Calculation: Suppliers, vendors, etc., report payment experiences to determine the score. Reduced scores indicate that payments have been constantly late.

Importance:

• **Vendor Relationships:** A high Paydex score makes it easier to negotiate favorable trade credit terms with suppliers.

• **Loan Approvals:** Lenders may take the Paydex score into account when assessing loan applications.

• **Business Credibility:** A favorable Paydex score signals financial responsibility to potential partners and investors.

Improvement Tips:

• **Pay Bills On Time:** Timely payments are the most direct way to keep a high Paydex score.

• **Establish Trade Credit:** Take part in transactions with vendors that report payment activity to D&B.

• **Monitor Your Score:** Regularly check your Paydex score to make sure it accurately reflects your payment history.

3. Experian Business Credit Score

Score Range: The score ranges from 1 to 100.
• **76 to 100:** Low risk of default.
• **51 to 75:** Medium risk; the business might have some payment problems.
• **1 to 50:** High risk; there's a greater likelihood of default.

Calculation Factors:
• **Payment History:** Timeliness of payments strongly influences the score.
• **Credit Utilization:** The amount of credit used is equivalent to credit limits.
• **Credit Balances:** Lower balances, equivalent to credit limits, are favorable.
• **Public Records:** Bankruptcies, liens, and judgments negatively affect the score.
• **Business Size and Age:** Older businesses with a longer credit history typically have higher scores.
• **Credit Inquiries:** Frequent inquiries can negatively affect the score.

Importance:
• **Credit Decisions:** A higher Experian score usually results in better loan terms.
• **Supplier Relationships**: Good credit can result in favorable terms for payments.

- **Business Credibility:** Improves the business's reputation in the industry.

Improvement Tips:
- **Pay Bills on Time:** Timely payments are important.
- **Manage Credit Utilization:** Avoid using all of your credit lines to keep utilization low.
- **Monitor Public Records:** Avoid and resolve negative public records quickly.
- **Regularly Check Your Report:** Dispute any errors that could lower your score.

Intelliscore Plus: This is a more detailed version of the **Experian Business Credit Score**, which ranges from 300 to 850. For in-depth credit analyses; it provides a comprehensive understanding of a company's credit risk.

4. Equifax Business Credit Score

Score Range: Usually, the range of the Equifax Business Credit Risk Score is 101 to 992. Lower credit risk is indicated by a higher score.

Types of Scores Provided by Equifax:
- **Equifax Business Credit Risk Score:** Estimates the likelihood of a serious delinquency within 12 months.
- **Equifax Payment Index:** Reflects the payment history of a business and ranges from 0 to 100.
- **Equifax Business Failure Score:** predicts a business's chance of failing in a year, with a range of 1,000 to 1,880.

Calculation Factors:
- **Payment History:** Timeliness of payments is an important factor.
- **Credit Utilization:** High utilization can negatively impact the score.
- **Company Size and Age:** Older, more established businesses generally have higher scores.
- **Public Records:** Negative records such as bankruptcies or liens lower the score.
- **Industry Risk:** The risk connected with the industry impacts the score.
- **Credit Inquiries:** Regular inquiries can indicate financial stress.

Importance:
- **Lender Decision-Making:** Impacts loan terms, interest rates, and approval decisions.
- **Supplier Relationships:** It aids in negotiating advantageous payment terms with suppliers.
- **Business Reputation:** A high score improves the business's reputation.

Improvement Tips:
- **Timely Payments:** Paying bills on time is important.
- **Manage Credit Utilization:** Remember—utilization is low, and balances are paid down.
- **Monitor Public Records**: Promptly resolve any negative records.
- **Maintain Accurate Information:** Make sure the business information is up-to-date.
- **Review and Dispute Errors:** Review your Equifax report for mistakes on a regular basis.

5. Small Business Financial Exchange (SBFE)

A nonprofit organization called the Small Business Financial Exchange (SBFE) collects and organizes credit information from participating financial institutions. Although SBFE doesn't provide scores, credit bureaus use its data to produce business credit reports and scores.

Key Points:
- **Membership-Based:** Composed of financial institutions that offer credit to small businesses.
- **Data Collection:** Members provide comprehensive credit information, such as loan performance and payment history.
- **Data Use:** Credit bureaus such as Experian, Equifax, and Dun & Bradstreet use the information to generate business credit reports and scores.

Impact on Small Businesses:
- **Creditworthiness:** SBFE data influences credit profiles, which in turn affect the ability to obtain credit.
- **Transparency:** Businesses can observe how SBFE data influences their credit scores but cannot directly access the data.

Certified Vendors:
- Major credit bureaus' ratings indirectly influence banking choices by incorporating SBFE data.

Advantages for Lenders:
- **Risk Mitigation:** Helps lenders evaluate the risk associated with lending to small businesses.
- **Industry Benchmarking:** Allows lenders to benchmark their portfolios in opposition to industry trends.

6. Most and Least Used Business Credit Scores

Most Used Business Credit Scores:
- **FICO SBSS (Small Business Scoring Service):** Frequently used by banks and the SBA to approve loans; especially important in establishing eligibility for SBA 7(a) loans.
- **Dun & Bradstreet Paydex Score:** Vendors and suppliers frequently use this to determine trade credit terms.
- **Experian Business Credit Score:** Widely used in a variety of financial products, having an impact on credit limits, interest rates, and loan approvals.

Least Used Business Credit Scores:
- **SBFE Data:** While SBFE data is an important contributor to major credit bureau scores, it is not a stand-alone score and is not as directly "used" in decision-making as other credit agency scores.
- **Equifax Business Credit Score:** Despite its importance, it typically works in conjunction with other scores and reports, which lessens its impact on its own.

7. How Business Credit Scores Affect Banking Decisions

Loan Approval:
- Business credit scores are one of the primary criteria used to approve loans. The approval procedure frequently uses FICO SBSS scores as the initial filter.

Interest Rates:
- Lower interest rates are typically the result of higher credit scores, which indicate less risk for lenders.

Credit Limits:
- Strong credit scores may allow for larger loans or credit limits, but lower scores may limit the availability of credit.

Loan Terms:
- A business's credit score impacts the total loan conditions, which include fees and repayment schedules.

Risk Assessment:
- Credit scores offer a quick, standardized method for assessing loan risk, which is important for regulatory compliance and portfolio management.

WHAT TO KNOW ABOUT GETTING APPROVALS:

When you're going for business funding, remember the number one data point that banks look at is your personal credit score. This is called a PG. (Personal Guarantor). The exception to this rule is if you have a company that makes over $5M a year with strong financials, and many large financial tradelines already registered on your business credit report. If this is not the case, they will look very closely at your personal credit profile. This is why clients with a thin credit profile who say, "I want to put everything in my business," do not have a clear understanding of how the process works.

As mentioned in *The Great American Credit Secret* (Book 1), in order for banks to trust you, they must see a history showing that you can successfully make payments on time. Banks largely use the mirror technique. Whatever it is that you want, they look to see your history. So if you want a business credit card, they will look at personal credit cards. If you have a limit of $300, they will probably give you a lower limit of $300-$3000. If you have a $28,000 limit, they will probably give you a $20,000-$100,000 credit limit on the business side. A lot of it also depends on your personal and business income as well as other items on the report.

When it comes to funding, here are the main things a bank will look at:

1. Installments. This includes a car, personal loan, mortgage, and similar items. These are what I call buying power because they are what make banks comfortable giving you higher limits.

2. Revolving Accounts. This includes credit cards and lines of credit; even a HELOC, in most cases, is considered revolving. Revolving accounts boost your credit score.

3. Derogatory Accounts. If you have missed payments within a two-year period, in most cases, you will get denied or have a low limit. The other option is you can get approved for a subprime credit card or loan. Examples are Credit One and One Main Financial. These are not the best options, but they do help to build if you have a new or a low credit score. The best option is to have NO NEGATIVE items on your credit report. Do whatever it takes to legally get any negative remarks overturned. Your future depends on it.

4. Credit Score. Most banks like to see a score of 680 or better. A higher score does not in itself equal more money.

I've had clients with 800 credit scores get denied or low limits.

5. Income. Banks will look at both your personal and business income. Remember, depending on the type of funding you are seeking, in most cases, you can include projected as well as household revenue. To learn more about this, refer to *The Great American Credit Secret* (Book 1).

6. Relationship with Institution. Some lenders require you to be a member, but most don't. In *The Great American Credit Secret* (Book 1), we covered Inner Banking Credit. When you have a relationship with the institution you are applying with, this improves your chances of approval.

7. Business Credit Score. Many banks will look at your business credit scores, but as ironic as it sounds, this is the least important factor in deciding whether you get approved or not. You can have no business credit score and still get approved.

8. Age of Business. The longer, the better! But again, you can open a new business this week and be approved for $100k in business funding by next week. Depends on how you do it.

The above list is in order of importance. Number 1 being the most important, and number 8 being the least important. However, it's good to have all 8 in order.

Now, let's talk about obtaining business funding WITHOUT them checking your personal credit profile. Many of you have watched those YouTube videos that say: "NO DOC LENDERS" or

"BUSINESS FUNDING WITH NO PG!" Well, this is partly true. Let me break down the truths and misconceptions behind this click-bait so you can understand the fine print.

If you go to ChatGPT and look up all the banks that offer "no credit pull" credit cards, you will get a long list.

Of those that are included on the list are:

- Divvy
- Brex
- Ramp
- Truist
- Capital on tap
- WF (secured)
- FNBO
- Amex

Here's some information that ChatGPT won't tell you that is super important:

All banks mitigate risks. If anyone could open up an LLC for $400 and get a bunch of business credit cards, everyone would do it if that were all it takes. So the next question becomes how do they mitigate the risk? What are the banks looking at when they only pull your EIN? What are the guidelines?

- Some of them will want to see your financials.
- Some of them will want to Know that you already have other established business credit or tradelines.
- Some will approve you without anything, but it will be store credit, meaning that you can buy products inside their store. So, for example, if it's Costco, then that means that you can shop at Costco only but not use it for other things.

- Some of it will have payback periods of 30 days, where whatever you spend, you need to pay back in full the same month.
- Some approvals might be like $300 or $500

Here's how you can increase your chances (or the limits):

Go to nav.com And register your business. Sign up for the NAV business boost. It's $120 for three months. Then, sign up for the SBSS, which is $10 per month.

That would improve your business credit scores on Experian business, SBFE, SBSS, Dun & Bradstreet, and Equifax commercial. This process normally only takes 30 days to go into effect after you have made the payment. We'll get more into this in the next chapter.

This will improve your business vendor credit, but please don't confuse this with regular business credit like financial lines. They are not the same. Business vendor credit is looked at kind of like an authorized user is looked at on your personal credit, but it still helps.

Some banks, like Navy Federal Credit Union, will seldom ask for paystubs if you have been a member for a while. So this is considered "NO DOC." So there is some truth to this.

CONCLUSION

Managing and understanding your business's credit scores is important for obtaining funding, gaining advantageous condi-tions, and establishing a solid credit standing. By becoming knowledgeable about the various types of business credit scores, including the SBSS, Paydex, Experian, and Equifax scores, as well as the role of the SBFE, you can take proactive steps to maintain and improve your credit standing and be in a better position to grow your business and achieve long-term success.

NINE
SETTING UP YOUR BUSINESS CREDIT PROFILE

Now, let's discuss one of the most important parts of managing a profitable company: creating a business credit profile. Although it may not sound as exciting as introducing a new product or sealing a major contract, your company credit profile can be the cherry on top of your financial reputation. If your company's credit profile is weak, you can still obtain loans, attract investors, and even negotiate advantageous terms with suppliers. Don't let anyone tell you otherwise. However, having good business credit will open up more doors and enhance your overall credit portfolio, and it's a lot easier to do than it sounds. Let's now explore how you may create and manage a strong business credit profile using AI tools and best practices.

THE IMPORTANCE OF A CREDIBILITY CHECK

Let's go over something fundamental again: credibility, before we go into the specifics of credit monitoring and AI technologies. Combining personal and corporate information is one of the top mistakes made by new business owners. And I understand—it's simple to believe that your firm can survive on your personal credit alone. Here's the point, though: you have to maintain everything distinct if you want your firm to be considered seriously. This calls for having a business phone number, business address, business website, and business email. You must register everything under the company's name.

What makes this so important? Banks, lenders, and other potential partners are assessing your company's trustworthiness and searching for professionalism and consistency. If your company uses Gmail instead of a domain name for business communications or if your business phone number is the same as your personal cell phone number, it raises red flags. It gives the impression that your company is less reputable and less established.

However, mingling personal and business information might negatively impact your creditworthiness, so it's not only a matter of perspective. For instance, any problems with your credit may have an immediate effect on your organization's capacity to obtain funding if you're using it to obtain commercial loans. For this reason, it's imperative that you draw a distinct line in the financials between your personal and commercial affairs from the outset. Also, much of your company's info is public information online. So, if, for any reason, you use your home address as your business address, the entire world will know where you live.

So, how do we put all of these to use? First things first, confirm that your personal and company bank accounts are distinct from one another. Make sure your business address appears consistently in all paperwork and online listings, and use this account for all business transactions. Invest in a professional email address and website. This will help you project credibility and legitimacy to banks and other financial organizations, so it's not just about looking good.

NAV: MONITORING PERSONAL CREDIT AS A BUSINESS OWNER

Now that we have established the importance of clearly separating personal and professional information, let's dive into the importance of closely monitoring your personal credit. "But isn't this about business credit?" one may wonder. Indeed. The truth is that, particularly in the beginning, your personal credit still has a big impact on the financial stability of your company. Read that again!

We present Nav, an essential tool for business owners who want to closely monitor their personal credit. Why is this relevant? This is relevant because many lenders may consider your personal credit score when determining the trustworthiness of your business. This is especially true if your company is brand new or doesn't currently have a strong credit history. In these situations, your personal credit represents your company's ability to repay loans or credit lines.

With Nav, you can monitor your personal and business credit, giving you a comprehensive understanding of your financial status. This AI-powered tool gathers data from the main credit bureaus to give you real-time credit score updates and warnings for any changes that might affect your creditworthiness.

However, observation is only the first step. Additionally, Nav provides tailored advice and insights on raising your credit score. For example, Nav may advise you to pay off your large credit card bills in order to raise your credit usage ratio, which is a crucial component in determining your credit score. You can improve your own credit score by implementing this AI-driven advice, which will help your company's financial reputation.

Don't overlook the significance of developing a solid business credit profile. As vital as your personal credit is, you should also create a distinct credit record for your company as soon as you can. Nav can also help with this by providing guidance on how to establish and improve your company credit. This includes advice on what business credit cards or loans to apply for, as well as tips on how to handle your company's money wisely in order to raise your credit score.

To put it briefly, Nav is the tool you should use to make sure your business and personal credit profiles are in excellent condition. You're positioning yourself for success when it comes time to apply for financing or negotiate better terms with suppliers if you maintain your credit and heed Nav's AI-driven suggestions. Nav also provides a bonus company tradeline enhancement. This allows you to submit a vendor tradeline to your credit report, which will improve your company score on Paydex, Experian Company, Equifax Commercial, and SBFE (little Business Financial Exchange)—all of which will increase with a little monthly payment from you (usually between $30 and $50). Additionally, it will raise your SBSS score for an extra $10. (Well worth the financial outlay!) And, to be honest, the SBSS scores are checked more often than you think. This is an easy win!

CREDIT GENIUS APP: STREAMLINING BUSINESS CREDIT BUILDING WITH AI

Let's dive into the Credit Genius App, also known as Credit Genius AI- a revolutionary tool for building and maintaining a strong personal and business credit profile, after discussing the fundamental principles of separating personal and business funds and monitoring your credit. Using artificial intelligence (AI), Credit Genius AI streamlines the entire process, making it simpler than ever to build, track, and enhance your business credit.

Therefore, what gives the Credit Genius App its power? First and foremost, the Credit Genius App caters specifically to business owners who want to manage their credit report. The app provides a number of features that walk you through the entire process of establishing credit and offer answers to all of your queries, including which particular bank to choose when applying for a loan. It can offer recommendations based on your information, objectives, and unique credit profile. It can also help you challenge erroneous data to eliminate it and enhance your score in various ways. For every entrepreneur, it is effectively a personal credit mentor. Best of all, it's free. However, there are improvements available for overachievers that you can take advantage of.

The AI-driven insights of the Credit Genius App are one of its most notable features. In addition to showing your credit score, the app offers insights into its factors and ways to improve it. For instance, the app may recommend paying off particular loans or settling on better terms with your creditors if it determines that you are carrying too much debt. Alternatively, the app may suggest obtaining a new line of credit to raise your score if it determines that you aren't using enough credit.

However, Credit Genius AI does more than just help you handle problems; it also supports you in actively establishing your credit. For example, the app can suggest specific suppliers or vendors who provide information to businesses and personal credit agencies, allowing you to earn credit points on each purchase. Additionally, the app can help you determine which business credit cards or loans, based on your current credit profile, have the highest approval rate when you apply for them.

The advantages don't end there. Additionally, the Credit Genius App provides real-time financial health monitoring features. This includes keeping tabs on your spending, managing your cash flow, and even projecting your future financial requirements. By closely monitoring your finances, you can make well-informed decisions that contribute to the long-term health and success of your company.

Credit Genius AI's capacity to assist you in obtaining better financial terms is among its most beneficial features. An excellent company credit profile increases your chances of approval for loans with better terms, greater credit limits, and cheaper interest rates. This can have a big impact on the financial health of your company, particularly if you expand and take on new tasks.

Continuous credit monitoring is crucial. You may take care of matters before they become problems by using the Credit Genius App, which provides real-time alerts for any changes in your business credit profile. By taking a proactive approach to credit management, you can make sure that your company is always in the best possible position to negotiate with suppliers, acquire funding, and expand operations.

BEST PRACTICES FOR BUILDING AND MAINTAINING BUSINESS CREDIT

After discussing the resources available to assist you in establishing and maintaining your company credit, let's discuss some best practices you should adhere to in order to guarantee long-term success. Recall that developing a solid company credit profile is a continuous process that calls for deliberate attention to detail and smart decision-making.

Above all, ensure that you always pay your bills on time. Although it may seem apparent, this is one of the most crucial elements in developing a solid credit profile. Late payments can significantly damage your credit score, making it more challenging for you to secure financing in the future. Set up reminders or automated payments to make sure you never forget a deadline.

Second, control the amount of debt your company has. Although using credit to establish your reputation is vital, having a high debt load can reduce your creditworthiness. Ensure you are not overextending yourself by monitoring your debt-to-income ratio. If you're having trouble managing your high debt levels, think about speaking with a financial advisor or creating a debt management strategy with the help of apps like the Credit Genius App.

Third, build credit with a variety of providers and vendors. The more accounts you have that report to commercial credit bureaus. To diversify your credit profile, make sure the vendors you work with are registered with major bureaus such as Dun & Bradstreet. You may also want to start accounts with new suppliers.

Fourth, examine your company's credit reports on a frequent basis. Errors occur, and having inaccuracies on your credit record might lower your score. Make use of tools such as Nav and the Credit Genius App to monitor your credit reports and dispute any inaccuracies. Maintaining your credit reports will ensure that your profile accurately portrays your company's financial standing.

The fifth step is to establish a relationship with your bank. Strong ties to your bank might lead to more advantageous terms and better financing possibilities. On a regular basis, meet with your bank to discuss your company's financial requirements and objectives, and be open and honest about your financial situation. When it comes time to apply for a loan or line of credit, having a positive connection with your bank might make all the difference.

Lastly, use consistency and patience. It takes time to establish a solid business credit profile, but the benefits are well worth the effort. Remain committed to upholding sound financial practices, and direct your efforts with the tools and techniques we've covered. You'll develop a credit profile over time that helps your company succeed and expand.

CONCLUSION: THE POWER OF A STRONG BUSINESS CREDIT PROFILE

Your credit profile is one of your most important assets in the corporate world. It's essential for getting funding, haggling for better terms with suppliers, and establishing a solid financial base for your company. However, it takes time, careful preparation, smart decision-making, and the appropriate resources to establish and maintain a solid credit profile.

You can take charge of your personal and business credit profiles and position yourself for long-term success by utilizing AI-driven tools like Nav and Credit Genius AI. Whether you're just starting out or trying to improve your current credit record, these tools provide the information and guidance you need to make wise decisions and build a solid financial future for your company.

But keep in mind that credibility is the foundation of everything. Keep your personal and corporate finances separate, maintain a professional online profile, and closely monitor your credit reports. Building a company credit profile that not only meets your immediate needs but also puts you in a position for future growth and success is possible if you adhere to these best practices and make use of the resources available to you.

So spend some time improving your company's credit profile. You'll be well on your way to creating a solid, reliable, and prosperous company that is prepared to prosper in the cutthroat business world of today with the appropriate strategy and resources.

TEN

BUSINESS CREDIT CARDS AND TRADE LINES

Your approach to business credit cards and trade lines is important for establishing and preserving business credit. These financial tools help you do more than simply get funding; they also help you get favorable conditions from lenders and establish your company's creditworthiness. In this chapter, we'll look at how AI-powered solutions like Hatchful by Shopify and Docracy may help you with credit terms negotiations, document management, and creating a strong brand identity that boosts funding prospects and your company's reputation.

DOCRACY: AI-POWERED LEGAL DOCUMENT MANAGEMENT

Let's begin with Docracy, an AI-powered software meant to assist you in creating and organizing legal papers. Making sure all of your legal paperwork is in place, including contracts and vendor agreements, is essential to keeping up excellent business credit. These agreements set the parameters for your business dealings and are critical to preserving your company's creditworthiness.

Docracy uses AI to streamline the production, administration, and storage of these legal documents. It offers customized templates and AI-generated documents to meet your specific needs, freeing you from the burden of legal phrasing and the hours spent crafting contracts. This guarantees that your contracts are lucid, compliant with the law, and consistent with the objectives of your company.

However, the benefits of document creation extend beyond this. Trade lines are essential credit accounts that provide information to company credit bureaus, and the platform assists you in managing them. You can better negotiate favorable credit conditions by maintaining organized and current agreements with suppliers and creditors. You may utilize Docracy to negotiate a net 60 term, for example, if a vendor provides a net 30 payment term but you've always made your payments on time. This will improve your cash flow without negatively affecting your credit score.

Docracy's AI-driven capabilities simplify the management of your company's legal aspects that directly impact your creditworthiness. Having the appropriate legal paperwork in place is crucial for fostering confidence with lenders and guaranteeing your company maintains its excellent standing, whether you're negotiating new loan conditions or preserving current trade lines.

HATCHFUL BY SHOPIFY: BUILDING A CONSISTENT BRAND IDENTITY

Next up is Hatchful by Shopify, an AI tool focused entirely on branding. You may be thinking, *What does branding have to do with business credit?* The response is everything. Building confidence with financial institutions and investors is just as important as enticing customers with a dependable, polished brand identity.

With Hatchful by Shopify, you can develop a unified brand identity that embodies the goals and values of your company. You can create logos, color schemes, and other brand aspects with AI-powered design tools to make sure your company has a consistent online presence across all platforms. This is important because having a strong, recognizable brand gives the impression that your company is more reputable and established, which may improve your creditworthiness.

Financial institutions consider more than just your company's financials when determining whether to grant you credit or provide funding; they also consider your company's general credibility. A clearly defined brand identity influences this impression by communicating your company's well-run, competent, and long-term success. As a result, lenders may feel more comfortable granting greater credit lines or better credit terms.

Furthermore, a strong brand identity can boost your marketing campaigns, increase sales, and strengthen your finances, all of which will improve your company's credit rating. Not only can Hatchful help your business seem beautiful, but it also paves the way for improved lending relationships and financial opportunities by helping you establish and manage a consistent brand.

CONCLUSION: LEVERAGING AI FOR BUSINESS CREDIT SUCCESS

In the world of business credit, every bit of information matters. This includes the legal documents that support your credit agreements, as well as your brand identity, which influences how lenders view your company. You may expedite these procedures and make sure your company is in a position to obtain favorable loan terms and establish a solid, reliable financial profile by utilizing AI solutions such as Hatchful by Shopify and Docracy.

By facilitating the management of your company's legal affairs, Docracy makes it simpler to establish and preserve trade lines that demonstrate your creditworthiness. Better funding opportunities and increased trust from financial institutions are made possible by Hatchful by Shopify, which makes sure your brand identity is consistent and professional.

By combining these AI-powered solutions, you can manage your company's credit profile in a complete way and confidently handle the complexity of credit cards, trade lines, and financial partnerships.

ELEVEN

APPLYING FOR FUNDING WITH AI

Whether you're an established corporation trying to grow or a startup seeking seed capital, obtaining funding is frequently the lifeblood of any business. However, navigating the funding landscape can be difficult due to the abundance of possibilities, intricate standards, and fierce rivalry. Herein lies the opportunity for AI to transform the way firms approach fundraising. We'll go into excellent detail in this chapter on how AI-powered tools, such as the Credit Genius App and CB Insights (which we talked about earlier), may help you find the best financing sources for your company, expedite the funding process, and make sure your plan is in line with investor preferences and market trends.

CREDIT GENIUS APP: NAVIGATING THE FUNDING LANDSCAPE WITH AI.

The world of funding can be confusing, with many turns, twists, and dead ends. The sheer number of alternatives available to entrepreneurs might be daunting, since they can range from conventional bank loans to grants, crowdsourcing, venture capital, and more. The issue is not just about raising money, but also about raising the right kind of money. The Credit Genius App solves that problem and changes the way companies look for funding.

UNDERSTANDING THE ROLE OF AI IN FUNDING

Credit Genius uses AI to assess your business's unique characteristics and match them with the best funding sources. This is no straightforward task, as AI takes into account a wide range of variables, such as the industry, size, revenue, credit profile, and growth potential of your company. The goal is to find finance options that complement your company's unique requirements while reducing the time, effort, and guesswork typically associated with obtaining capital.

For example, AI might advise you to check into venture capital firms that specialize in early-stage tech startups if you're a tech startup with a strong business strategy but little income. On the other hand, if you run a small retail business, AI can direct you to government subsidies or alternative lenders if your company has consistent cash flow but a low credit score. Businesses similar to yours are the target audience for these programs.

In addition to its enormous processing and analysis capacity, artificial intelligence (AI) can find funding opportunities you may not have even realized existed. This broadens your funding possibilities and improves your chances of locating the ideal fit, be it an angel investment, a small company loan, or something entirely else.

STREAMLINING THE APPLICATION PROCESS

Collecting the necessary documentation and completing several applications is one of the most time-consuming parts of the financing application process. Because every lender or investor has different requirements, there may be a ton of paperwork and a large time commitment. The Credit Genius App streamlines this process by automating numerous tedious tasks.

By utilizing artificial intelligence (AI), the app can reduce the amount of human data entry required by pre-filling applications with information you've already submitted. Additionally, it assists you in gathering and arranging the required paperwork, including credit reports, company plans, and financial records, so that everything is in order before you submit your applications.

However, the software offers more than simply automation; it also offers suggestions and insights that can improve your applications. For example, if the AI may recommend changes or more documentation to improve your chances of approval if it finds that your business plan is vague in some areas or that your financial projections are insufficient. This kind of proactive advice can really help, especially if you're in a competitive market for scarce capital with other businesses.

MATCHING WITH THE RIGHT FUNDING SOURCES

The Credit Genius App's true strength is its capacity to link your company with the best funding sources. Applying for funding from every source and hoping that anything sticks is a shotgun approach. Instead, the app leverages artificial intelligence (AI) to find the best connections based on the characteristics of your business.

Let's take an example of a growing business with excellent revenue but little cash flow. The app can match you with lenders who specialize in credit lines or working capital loans, designed to help companies manage their cash flow during periods of rapid expansion. However, if your company is focused on technology and innovation, the app may connect you with angel or venture capital firms looking for high-potential businesses.

Since the matching process is dynamic, it considers investor preferences and market trends in addition to your present financial status. This ensures that your funding applications are submitted to the right funding sources at the right time. For example, the AI may give priority to certain possibilities in its recommendations if it notices that a venture capital company is actively seeking investments in your industry or that a specific lender has recently relaxed its lending conditions.

The Credit Genius app greatly improves your chances of finding the cash you need for your business by utilizing artificial intelligence (AI). Additionally, it shortens the time and effort needed to locate and submit an application for funding, freeing you up to concentrate on managing your company instead of looking for capital.

LEVERAGING AI INSIGHTS TO SECURE BETTER TERMS

An important stage in the fundraising process is negotiating the terms. Your company's financial health can be greatly impacted by the terms of a loan or investment, even if you are approved for one. These factors include ownership stakes, interest rates, and repayment plans. Using artificial intelligence, the Credit Genius App helps you negotiate better terms by assessing the offers you receive and providing advice on how to bargain. Recall that everything depends on the questions you ask; describe your circumstances, and it will examine your credit report to provide you with an answer.

For example, if you receive a loan with a high interest rate, the AI can advise you to negotiate for a lower rate based on your excellent credit history, or it can provide you with information about other lenders who might be able to offer better conditions.

In a similar vein, the software may assist you in determining a reasonable business valuation and offer tactics for holding onto more equity if you're in negotiations with investors. Recall that it is free.

The AI also monitors market trends and industry benchmarks to make sure you're not just taking the first offer you come across but instead making wise decisions that support your long-term objectives. This degree of research and direction can have a big impact, especially for company owners who are inexperienced with financing or have never negotiated before.

CB INSIGHTS: ALIGNING YOUR FUNDING STRATEGY WITH MARKET TRENDS

CB Insights uses artificial intelligence (AI) to examine market trends and industry data more comprehensively, while Credit Genius focuses on connecting your business with appropriate funding sources. For companies looking to match investor preferences and market conditions with their funding strategy, this tool is especially helpful.

UNDERSTANDING THE MARKET LANDSCAPE WITH AI

CB Insights is a useful tool for examining the competitive landscape and identifying trends that could affect your fundraising plan. With the use of artificial intelligence (AI), the platform analyzes enormous volumes of data, including investor activity, market research, and financial reports, to provide you with a thorough understanding of the financing landscape.

For instance, CB Insights can assist you in determining which biotech subfields are now drawing the greatest investment if you work in the biotech sector. Do investors prefer to back health technology, medical equipment, or medication development?

Which new developments have the potential to influence the sector in the upcoming years? Aligning your funding plan with investor objectives and understanding the market's direction can enhance your chances of securing financing.

CB Insights' AI-driven insights enable you to recognize possible hazards and possibilities in your sector. For example, if the AI notices that a lot of investors are leaving a certain industry, it may advise you to diversify your sources of funding or look into other businesses where investment is increasing. Using a proactive approach, you can ensure that your company stays ahead of the curve and that investors continue to find it appealing.

IDENTIFYING THE BEST BANKS AND LENDERS FOR YOUR BUSINESS

CB Insights is also important in finding the best banks and lenders for your company. The platform assists you in identifying the financial institutions that are most likely to satisfy your needs by analyzing data on lender activity, loan conditions, and approval rates.

For example, CB Insights may help small firms in the retail industry find banks with a favorable history of lending to other retailers. Additionally, it might draw attention to lenders who are currently providing advantageous terms, such as longer payback durations or lower interest rates.

You can improve your chances of getting money and better conditions by concentrating your efforts on the most qualified lenders.

Additionally, CB Insights offers information on the kinds of companies that each lender generally deals with. When creating your funding applications, this can be really helpful because it lets you adjust your pitch to fit the needs and preferences of the lender. For example, you may highlight your company's sustainability activities in your application if the lender has a history of backing eco-friendly firms.

ALIGNING YOUR FUNDING STRATEGY WITH INVESTOR PREFERENCES

CB Insights is a useful tool for evaluating investor preferences in addition to researching banks and lenders. It's critical to understand what investors want, whether you're searching for private equity, venture capital, or angel funding.

CB Insights uses artificial intelligence (AI) to evaluate data on investor activity, including the sectors they invest in, the types of companies they support, and the phases of development they prioritize. This lets you identify potential investors and tailor your pitch to their preferences.

For instance, CB Insights can help a tech startup create a novel AI-powered platform and find venture capital companies that have previously made investments in related technology. Additionally, it could draw attention to investors who have a specific interest in startups with promising growth prospects. With this knowledge at hand, you can create a proposal that specifically addresses the needs of these investors, improving your chances of getting finance.

With CB Insights, you can also gain insight into wider market trends that may affect investor choices. For example, even if sustainability isn't your main focus, AI may recommend emphasizing your company's environmentally friendly features if it senses that interest in sustainable technologies is expanding. You may attract more investors to your firm and improve your chances of raising funding by coordinating your pitch with current market trends.

LEVERAGING DATA TO MAKE INFORMED FUNDING DECISIONS

The ultimate goal of using CB Insights is to make well-informed funding decisions that complement your company's demands and the state of the industry. Using the platform's AI-driven insights, you can target the best banks and lenders, find the best funding sources, and create proposals that appeal to investors.

Additionally, CB Insights offers continuous monitoring and analysis, enabling you to stay abreast of market developments and modify your funding plan as necessary. In today's fast-paced business climate, when conditions can change quickly, and new possibilities might surface at any time, this level of awareness and flexibility is essential.

You could stay ahead of the market by incorporating CB Insights into your funding plan rather than just responding to it. This proactive strategy can give your company a significant competitive advantage and put you in the best position to get the funding you need to expand and prosper.

BEST PRACTICES FOR APPLYING FOR FUNDING WITH AI

After going over the Potent features of the Credit Genius App and CB Insights, let's discuss some recommended practices for utilizing AI to submit funding applications. By following these guidelines, you can make the most of these resources and ensure that your funding applications are as competitive as possible.

1. Start Early and Plan Ahead
Businesses often make the mistake of delaying seeking capital until they are severely cash-strapped. Starting early and utilizing AI tools such as CB Insights and the Credit Genius App will help you create a well-thought-out fundraising plan that fits your company's objectives and

the state of the industry. By preparing ahead of time, you can improve your credit score, polish your business plan, and obtain the required paperwork before you start the application process.

2. Use AI to Personalize Your Applications

Artificial intelligence (AI) solutions such as the Credit Genius App and CB Insights offer useful insights into the requirements of investors and lenders. Utilize this data to tailor your applications and pitches, emphasizing the parts of your company that correspond with the require-ments of each financing source. You will significantly increase your chances of acceptance by tailoring your applications to highlight your market traction, environ-mental initiatives, or development prospects.

3. Monitor Market Trends Continuously

The funding landscape is ever-changing, with new possi-bilities and trends appearing on a regular basis. Employing AI tools like CB Insights to continuously track market trends can help you stay ahead of the curve and make necessary adjustments to your fundraising plan. You may find new funding sources, steer clear of possible dangers, and seize new opportunities by being proactive.

4. Leverage AI to Negotiate Better Terms

Instead of blindly accepting the first offer you receive, use AI to evaluate the terms and negotiate better deals. The terms you accept will have a lasting effect on the financial stability of your company, regardless of whether you're seeking a loan or obtaining an investment. Artificial intel-ligence (AI) solutions, like the Credit Genius App, can offer insights about reasonable terms and how to bargain for more favorable rates, reduced fees, or payback schedules.

5. Keep Your Financials in Order

Lastly, before you begin seeking money, make sure your finances are in order. This entails keeping up-to-date financial records, skillfully handling cash flow, and routinely checking your credit report. By presenting a compelling case to lenders and investors and utilizing AI-driven solutions to monitor your finances, you can enhance your chances of securing the necessary funding.

THE FUTURE OF FUNDING IS AI-DRIVEN

The world of business financing is complex, competitive, and constantly changing. However, armed with the appropriate resources and tactics, you can confidently negotiate this terrain and obtain the funding your company requires to prosper. AI-driven tools like the Credit Genius App and CB Insights are revolutionizing the way businesses approach finance by simplifying the identification of appropriate sources, speeding up the application process, and aligning your strategy with market trends.

By implementing these resources, you're setting up your company for long-term success, in addition to improving your chances of obtaining money. AI may help you navigate the funding market more skillfully and make decisions that support your organization's expansion and growth, whether you're an established firm looking to expand or a startup looking for seed cash.

Therefore, leverage AI's potential in your financing plan. By utilizing the appropriate tools and approach, you can turn the difficult and often intimidating process of obtaining money into a smart and efficient undertaking that positions your company for success in today's competitive and fast-paced industry.

TWELVE
SCALING YOUR OPERATIONS

All of your hard work will pay off when you grow your business; you'll be able to reach a wider audience, generate more income, and develop a solid reputation for yourself rather than just existing in the market. But scaling is one of the hardest phases in a business's life cycle. Increasing the amount of what you presently do is not enough to achieve strategic growth in a way that is both sustainable and meets market expectations. This is where artificial intelligence (AI) enters the picture. It offers powerful tools that can predict shifts in the market, identify opportunities for growth, and help you implement growth strategies properly. This chapter will cover how you can effectively scale your business to ensure sustainable and strategic growth with the use of AI-powered tools like Trend Hunter and Bizplan.

TREND HUNTER: CAPITALIZING ON SCALING OPPORTUNITIES WITH AI

First up, let's look into Trend Hunter, an AI-powered platform focused on staying ahead of the curve. Timing is important when it comes to growing your business. Overextension, financial pressure, and even corporate failure can result from expanding too quickly or in the wrong direction. On the other hand, losing market share to more nimble rivals can result from passing on a scaling opportunity. Here's where Trend Hunter comes in: by forecasting changes in the industry and in consumer behavior, it uses AI to help you find and seize scaling possibilities.

UNDERSTANDING MARKET SHIFTS WITH AI

Selecting the right time and location for expansion is one of the biggest problems with growing. Global trends, shifting customer tastes, and advancements in technology all contribute to the ongoing evolution of markets. What's popular today can become outdated tomorrow, and companies that don't adjust risk falling behind their competitors. Trend Hunter, using artificial intelligence (AI), analyzes a ton of data, including industry publications and social media trends, to provide you with a real-time picture of the market's direction.

Let's say, for instance, that you manage a direct-to-consumer (DTC) business that sells environmentally friendly goods. Trend Hunter's AI may analyze data demonstrating an increasing customer interest in eco-friendly packaging options. This understanding may indicate a chance to grow your business by adding more environmentally friendly product packaging to your lineup or stepping up your marketing to draw attention to how sustainable your offerings are. By implementing these ideas, you're not only growing your company, but also positioning yourself as a leader in a new industry.

However, Trend Hunter does more than just point out trends; it also explains how these patterns relate to your particular business model and industry. With the help of the platform's AI tools, you can leverage market shifts to gain actionable insights that are pertinent to your organization and make well-informed decisions about where to allocate your resources. Trend Hunter provides you with the data-driven confidence to scale strategically, whether you're increasing manufacturing, entering new markets, or introducing a new product line.

EXAMPLES OF BUSINESSES THAT SCALED WITH AI INSIGHTS

Let's examine a few actual cases of companies that effectively expanded their operations by utilizing AI insights from Trend Hunter and other platforms. These businesses not only grew, but also evolved intelligently by employing AI to manage the challenges of growing in a cutthroat industry.

Consider a fashion retailer that increased the scope of its product offering by leveraging AI-driven insights. Through an analysis of industry trends and consumer behavior, the company found that there was an increasing demand for sustainable, ethically sourced clothes. The company took this insight and, instead of continuing with its current product line, launched a new line of sustainable fashion. What was the outcome? In addition to satisfying a growing consumer need, the business established itself as a pioneer in sustainable fashion, which resulted in a notable increase in sales.

Another example comes from the tech industry, where a software provider employed AI to spot a need in the market for solutions for small businesses. With the use of Trend Hunter's AI capabilities, the business was able to examine consumer feedback and market data using Trend Hunter's AI capabilities, uncovering an underserved market of small enterprises in need of scalable, reasonably priced software. In response, the business created a line of items specifically designed for this market, which sped up its growth and greatly increased its market share.

These illustrations show how AI can effectively direct decisions about scale. Businesses can make sure that their scaling efforts are not just effective but long-lasting by using AI insights to find the right opportunities at the right time.

BIZPLAN: PLANNING AND EXECUTING SCALING STRATEGIES WITH AI

The next step after identifying a scaling opportunity is to properly prepare and carry out your approach. Bizplan, a full-featured AI-driven tool, assists you in precisely mapping out and implementing scaling strategies. Scaling is about managing growth in a way that is sustainable and in line with your long-term objectives. It's not just about expanding into new markets or boosting production. With Bizplan, you can organize all the elements of your scaling initiatives, from resource allocation to financial forecasts, and make sure you're ready for the opportunities and difficulties that come with growth.

CRAFTING A DATA-DRIVEN SCALING PLAN

Successful scaling requires a thorough data-driven plan. You must determine the cost of scaling, the best place to allocate resources, and the potential return on investment. The AI tools from Bizplan streamline this process by examining your company's financial information, industry dynamics, and growth potential to help you create a thorough scaling strategy.

Bizplan, for example, could help you estimate the costs associated with expanding into a new geographic market, including supply chain logistics and marketing expenditures. The AI technologies on the platform can also assess the market's state in a new area, assisting you in choosing the most efficient launch window and marketing tactics. By offering comprehensive financial estimates and growth scenarios, Bizplan ensures that you're not just speculating, but rather making well-informed decisions based on reliable data.

With Bizplan, you can also prepare for the operational challenges that come with scaling. Your business's management challenges will increase as it expands. It is important to make sure that your infrastructure is prepared for an increase in demand, that your personnel are capable of taking on more responsibilities, and that your procedures are expandable. With Bizplan's AI technologies, you can identify potential inefficiencies and bottlenecks and take action to fix them before they worsen.

CONTINUOUS MONITORING AND ADJUSTMENT WITH AI

It's a fact that losing control of your business operations is one of the main risks of scaling. As your company expands, it's easy to feel overburdened by the amount of work and obligations. As a result, effective scalability necessitates constant observation and modification, and this is where Bizplan's AI capabilities truly shine.

In addition to assisting with the planning of your scaling initiatives, Bizplan provides continuous monitoring and insights to ensure your growth's sustainability. The platform's AI technologies continuously evaluate the success of your company and notify you in real time of any potential problems or possibilities. This enables you to make changes as needed, keeping your growing initiatives on course.

For example, Bizplan may recommend modifying your scaling timetable or obtaining more finance to sustain your growth if it notices that your quick expansion is placing a burden on your cash flow. Alternatively, the platform may suggest adjusting your marketing tactics to increase effectiveness if it detects an increase in your customer acquisition costs. With its real-time insights and recommendations, Bizplan gives you the confidence to success- fully handle the challenges of growth.

Bizplan also emphasizes the importance of scenario planning. This involves making plans for potential outcomes depending on a range of variables, such as shifts in consumer behavior, competing actions, or market conditions. With the help of the platform's AI technologies, you can model alternative growth scenarios and assess how your company would fare in different circumstances. This kind of insight is priceless because it allows you to see obstacles ahead of time and modify your plan of action before they negatively affect your profitability.

AVOIDING POTENTIAL PITFALLS WITH AI

There are many potential risks when scaling, such as overex- tending your resources or misestimating consumer demand. However, by using AI-powered solutions like Bizplan, you may scale more successfully and steer clear of these typical blunders.

One of the biggest risks during scaling is losing focus on your primary business. As your company grows, it's easy to lose sight of the things that initially made it successful in favor of new ventures. By regularly monitoring your core company activities and making sure that your scaling efforts don't jeopardize your current business, Bizplan's AI technologies assist you in main- taining focus.

Underestimating the costs associated with scalability is another common mistake. Scaling frequently necessitates a large financial outlay, whether it's for marketing in a new area, expanding your workforce, or updating your technology. Bizplan's AI-driven financial planning tools enable businesses to ensure they have the resources required to sustain their growth and accurately estimate these expenses.

Finally, Bizplan helps you manage the human aspect of scaling. Your staff expands along with your firm, and managing a larger workforce has its own set of challenges. In order to make sure that your workforce is prepared to tackle the demands of a growing firm, Bizplan's AI tools can help you plan for this by analyzing your staffing needs, finding skill gaps, and even offering training programs.

CONCLUSION: SCALING WITH CONFIDENCE USING AI

One of the most exciting and challenging stages of business growth is scaling. While there are many opportunities at this time, it's also critical to plan ahead carefully, make wise decisions, and keep a close eye on things. You can confidently negotiate the challenges of scaling using AI-driven tools like Trend Hunter and Bizplan, making sure that your growth is both sustainable and strategic.

Trend Hunter's ability to predict market and customer behavior changes allows you to spot and seize growth opportunities. Using AI insights, you can decide when and where to grow, ensuring that your scaling initiatives are in line with the state of the industry.

With Bizplan's tools, you can successfully develop and implement your scaling strategy. Bizplan's AI-driven platform meticulously manages and tracks every aspect of your growth, from financial forecasts to scenario planning, helping you steer clear of potential pitfalls and steer your scaling efforts in the right direction.

When combined, these techniques provide a thorough, data-driven, strategic, and long-term success-oriented approach to growing. By incorporating AI into your scaling strategy, you're not only expanding your company, but also laying the groundwork for long-term, sustainable growth that will ensure its success.

So, as you grow your business, acknowledge AI's potential. With the appropriate tools and tactics, you can transform scaling obstacles into growth opportunities and move your company ahead with assurance and accuracy in a market that is constantly evolving.

THIRTEEN
OVERCOMING CHALLENGES WITH AI

Whether it's handling unpredictable cash flow, overcoming operational obstacles, or figuring out how to keep a solid credit profile, running a business is full of challenges. Though they are unavoidable, these difficulties don't have to be insurmountable. You can foresee, navigate, and even convert these obstacles into chances for personal development if you have the appropriate tools and tactics—especially those driven by artificial intelligence. In this chapter, we'll look at how AI-powered tools such as QuickBooks and Exploding Topics may help you keep up with market trends, handle your money wisely, and get beyond typical business obstacles—particularly those pertaining to credit and operational effectiveness.

EXPLODING TOPICS: STAYING AHEAD OF INDUSTRY TRENDS TO OVERCOME CHALLENGES

First up, let's look at Exploding Topics, an AI-driven platform that helps you stay ahead of the curve by seeing new trends before they catch on. Being aware of industry developments entails more than just keeping up with the latest fashions; it also entails spotting market shifts that may affect your company and being prepared to respond before problems arise.

LEVERAGING AI TO ANTICIPATE AND OVERCOME CHALLENGES

One of the biggest challenges businesses experience is the ongoing change in consumer behavior and market needs. Technologies and trends are constantly evolving, and strategies that were effective in the past may not be effective in the future. If you're not ready, this could cause problems with credit and operations. Using artificial intelligence (AI), Exploding Topics examines a ton of data from the internet, including social media, search engines, news sources, and more, to pinpoint trends that are picking up steam.

Let's say you work in retail, and Exploding Topics reports that customers are increasingly interested in subscription-based services. Early detection of this trend gives you the opportunity to change your company strategy to include subscription choices, keeping you ahead of the competition and fostering strong client loyalty. By taking a proactive approach, you can avoid the operational difficulties caused by declining sales or out-of-date business strategies.

But what does this have to do with getting over credit difficulties? As a result, staying ahead of any financial troubles also entails staying ahead of industry trends. You can prevent overstock and the associated cash flow problems, for example, by modifying your inventory and marketing methods in response to a trend indicating a decline in demand for a specific product line. This kind of foresight helps to maintain financial stability, which improves your company's credit profile.

AI-DRIVEN SOLUTIONS TO COMMON BUSINESS CREDIT ISSUES

Finding trends is only one aspect of Exploding Topics; applying such insights to practical challenges, such as typical company financing concerns, is another. Assume for the moment that your company is having trouble with high credit use as a result of your heavy reliance on credit to finance operations. By using Exploding Topics' ability to identify potential new income sources or cost-cutting measures, you can enhance your financial health and reduce your dependence on borrowing.

For example, you may look into ways to save costs by reducing your actual office space or implementing more flexible work arrangements if the platform detects a trend toward remote work and lower overhead costs. These changes can improve your company's credit profile by lowering credit utilization, increasing cash flow, and freeing up credit.

Additionally, by keeping up with market developments, you might foresee possible credit difficulties before they materialize. For example, you can act proactively to get finance or renegotiate terms before conditions worsen if a pattern signals tightening credit markets or rising interest rates. The long-term financial stability and creditworthiness of your company depend on this kind of proactive management.

QUICKBOOKS: AI-POWERED FINANCIAL MANAGEMENT FOR CREDIT STABILITY

Let's move on to the topic of QuickBooks, a financial management application that is now essential for companies of all kinds. Today's QuickBooks, however, is an AI-powered platform that assists you in preserving a healthy cash flow, guarding against credit problems, and guaranteeing your financial security. It is more than just accounting software. QuickBooks provides the information and tools you need to keep on top of your finances in a world where cash flow issues are one of the main causes of business failure.

PREVENTING CREDIT ISSUES WITH AI-DRIVEN FINANCIAL MANAGEMENT

Maintaining a healthy cash flow is one of the best strategies to avoid credit problems. Improper cash flow management can lead to a variety of issues, such as late payments, excessive credit usage, and, ultimately, a tarnished credit history. QuickBooks employs artificial intelligence (AI) to provide proactive suggestions and real-time insights into your financial health, allowing you to manage your cash flow more efficiently.

For example, QuickBooks has the ability to forecast your cash flow based on past performance, impending costs, and anticipated income. The AI may offer methods to reduce the likelihood of a cash shortage in the upcoming months, such as modifying your terms of payment with clients, obtaining a short-term loan, or reducing non-essential spending. By taking care of these problems before they get out of hand, you can avoid the cash flow problems that frequently result in late payments and credit problems.

QuickBooks helps you manage your accounts payable and receivable to prevent unexpected expenses or late payments. The platform's AI technologies enable you to automatically remind your customers to pay, ensuring timely payments and a steady income stream. Furthermore, QuickBooks can recommend the best times for you to pay your own bills, striking a balance between the necessity to keep good supplier connections and cash flow preservation.

By using AI-driven solutions to manage your finances, you actively contribute to the development of a stronger, more robust organization rather than just avoiding credit problems. A strong credit profile is essential for preserving financial stability, which in turn creates more chances for development and expansion.

THE IMPORTANCE OF PROACTIVE FINANCIAL MANAGEMENT

QuickBooks gives you the resources you require to manage your money well, but it's important to keep in mind that proactive financial management aims to position your company for success rather than just averting issues. Being in charge of your finances and cash flow puts you in a better position to seize opportunities, whether they include growing your business, acquiring new equipment, or negotiating better terms with suppliers.

With QuickBooks' AI-driven insights, you can confidently make these strategic decisions. For example, if the platform determines that your cash flow is continuously high, it may recommend looking at expansion prospects like taking on new projects or entering new markets. If the AI detects financial risks, it can notify you so you can act before they hurt your profits.

Maintaining your company's credit requires this degree of proactive monitoring. When lenders and creditors perceive that you manage your finances, they are more inclined to provide you with favorable terms and larger credit limits. As a result, you will have the financial freedom to expand your company without going overboard or compromising your credit.

BUILDING FINANCIAL RESILIENCE WITH AI

Utilizing AI-powered options, such as QuickBooks, should ultimately lead to the development of financial resilience—the ability of your company to withstand market fluctuations and preserve a solid credit standing. Financial resilience is the ability to thrive in the face of adversity and emerge from it stronger than simply getting by with it.

QuickBooks helps you develop resilience by providing an accurate, up-to-date picture of your financial situation and practical advice on how to strengthen it. The artificial intelligence technologies of the platform aim to assist your organization in preserving long-term financial stability, be it through enhancing cash flow, reducing unnecessary expenses, or discovering fresh revenue streams.

You are actively laying the groundwork for long-term success and growth by incorporating QuickBooks into your day-to-day business operations. This goes beyond simply managing your accounts. By taking a proactive approach to financial management, you can make sure that your company is creditworthy, strong, and prepared to take advantage of new possibilities as they present themselves.

CONCLUSION: OVERCOMING CHALLENGES WITH AI-DRIVEN SOLUTIONS

Every business faces difficulties, whether it's managing credit risks, keeping up with industry trends, or keeping a steady cash flow. However, if you employ the appropriate techniques and resources, you can overcome these challenges and even use them as opportunities for personal development. AI-driven platforms such as QuickBooks and Exploding Topics provide strong solutions to assist you in navigating these obstacles with accuracy and assurance.

By seeing new trends and offering useful advice on how to handle possible credit and operational issues, Exploding Topics helps you stay ahead of the curve. You may avoid financial troubles, adjust to market changes, and preserve a good credit profile by being proactive and knowledgeable.

On the other hand, QuickBooks provides all-inclusive financial management solutions that support sound cash flow management, credit dispute avoidance, and the development of financial resilience. QuickBooks provides proactive suggestions and real-time insights to help you take charge of your finances and set up your company for long-term success.

Together, these AI-powered solutions offer a comprehensive plan for conquering the obstacles that any company encounters. By utilizing AI to keep up with trends, handle money wisely, and develop financial resilience, you're not just surviving but thriving in a market that is becoming more and more competitive. So, embrace the ability of AI to overcome difficulties and watch as your company not only overcomes them but also uses them as an opportunity for expansion and success.

CONCLUSION
THE FUTURE OF BUSINESS CREDIT IN THE AGE OF AI

We've learned that the business credit management market is changing quickly as we've navigated its complexities. The era characterized by the revolutionary force of artificial intelligence (AI) is coming, replacing the days of relying exclusively on manual processes and traditional ways. AI is becoming more and more necessary, regardless of whether you're a startup trying to get off the ground or an established company aiming to grow. It is the key to managing your business credit and overall financial well-being in a smarter, quicker, and more efficient manner.

FINAL THOUGHTS

Throughout this book, we have explored many different aspects of AI's role in company credit management. We've looked at how AI can help you keep ahead of market trends, manage your finances with unmatched precision, and simplify the challenging process of obtaining funding. The message is clear: artificial intelligence (AI) is altering the way businesses approach credit and finance. Examples of this include the Credit Genius App's ability to match your business with the correct funding sources and QuickBooks' AI-driven financial insights.

Each chapter explores a deeper concept, however, which goes beyond the tools and technologies: AI aims to improve rather than merely simplify tasks. It's about providing you with the tools you need to turn data-driven insights into more intelligent decisions, enabling you to navigate the financial landscape with assurance and clarity. Artificial intelligence isn't simply a tool for the future; it's here and changing the corporate landscape in ways that were unthinkable only a few years ago.

This transformation has huge possibilities for businesses of all sizes. Budget constraints can sometimes limit small businesses, but AI can help them compete on an equal footing with larger corporations. Small businesses may get the credit and funding they require to expand and succeed by automating repetitive processes, learning about market trends, and making wise judgments.

AI presents a chance for established businesses to improve and streamline current tactics. It makes it possible to forecast more accurately, manage risks more effectively, and respond swiftly to shifting market conditions. Artificial intelligence (AI) offers the agility required to stay ahead of the competition and uphold a solid credit profile in a world where business is moving at an accelerated speed.

LOOKING AHEAD

So, what does the future hold for business credit in the age of AI? Continuous learning, adaptability, and a readiness to welcome change are the keys to the solution. AI will develop further, and with it will come the tools and approaches that enterprises may use. The people who stay ahead of the curve and make the investment to understand and apply AI to their operations will be the ones who, in the years to come, not only survive but prosper.

But where do you start? Here are some actionable steps to begin incorporating AI into your business credit strategy:

1. Assess Your Current Tools and Processes: Examine the resources you are currently using to manage your company's credit and finances.
Do they have AI capabilities installed? If not, think about switching to platforms like QuickBooks, the Credit Genius App, or others discussed in this book. These resources can yield quick gains in productivity and understanding.

2. Educate Yourself and Your Team: Artificial intelligence is a strong tool, but its efficacy depends on its users. Spend some time studying how AI is used in company finance. Motivate your group to follow suit. The more you know, the better you can use AI.

3. Start Small, Then Scale: If artificial intelligence (AI) is new to you, begin by implementing it in one aspect of your company, like financial management or trend analysis. If you're comfortable with its functionality, gradually incorporate AI into more aspects of your company's operations. With this method, you can achieve noticeable successes and gain confidence without becoming overwhelmed.

4. Stay Updated on AI Developments: AI is a field that is always changing, with new tools and capabilities appearing on a regular basis. Know the latest AI advances and consider how your company can benefit. This may be networking with other business owners who are employing AI, attending webinars, or subscribing to industry newsletters.

5. Embrace Continuous Improvement: The incorporation of artificial intelligence into your business's credit strategy is an ongoing process as opposed to a one-time event. Regularly assess and refine your AI-driven plans to ensure they align with your business goals and the dynamic market conditions. In the AI era, businesses committed to innovation and continuous development will prosper.

Remember, artificial intelligence (AI) should enhance human interaction in business, not take its place. You can make better, more informed decisions that propel your company toward greater success by fusing your business savvy with AI-driven insights. Artificial intelligence (AI) will drive businesses and business credit in general in the future, putting those who accept this fact in a strong position to lead. Thus, start implementing AI into your business credit plan right now. You have the resources, information, and power to change the future. You have endless opportunities for success, growth, and innovation when AI is on your side.

www.ingramcontent.com/pod-product-compliance
Lightning Source LLC
Chambersburg PA
CBHW060617210326
41520CB00010B/1377